YOUR HOME BUSINESS

Also by Helen Chryssides

Local Heroes, published by Collins Dove, a division of HarperCollins
A Different Light, published by HarperCollins

YOUR HOME BUSINESS

The essential guide to running your business from home

Helen Chryssides

ALLEN & UNWIN

First published in 1997 by
Allen & Unwin
9 Atchison Street
St Leonards NSW 2065
Australia
Phone: (61 2) 9901 4088
Fax: (61 2) 9906 2218
E-mail: frontdesk@allen-unwin.com.au
URL: http://www.allen-unwin.com.au

National Library of Australia
Cataloguing-in-Publication entry:

Chryssides, Helen.
Your home business: the essential guide to running your business from home.

ISBN 1 86448 306 7.

1. Home-based businesses—Management. 2. New business enterprises. I. Title.

658.041

Set in 10.5/12 pt Garamond by DOCUPRO, Sydney
Printed by Australian Print Group, Maryborough, Vic.

10 9 8 7 6 5 4 3 2 1

Dedicated to all home-based workers

CONTENTS

ACKNOWLEDGEMENTS

I would like to thank the home-based workers and all those who gave so willingly and generously of their time to share their experiences and expertise for the purposes of this book. Your comments and your wisdom are much appreciated and I congratulate you all on your commitment and dedication. My gratitude also goes to my ever patient, always optimistic and laterally thinking agent Margaret Connolly whose ability to combine home-based work and family life herself is truly inspiring.

I am grateful to Andrew Matthews for giving me permission to reproduce his fax sheet, which appears on page 99. I would also like to thank Andrew Weldon for his cartoons, which appear throughout the book.

My aim in writing this book has been to produce one that offers practical guidelines together with moral support.

This is the book I would have liked to have read when I was contemplating a home-based business many years ago—one that provided no-nonsense information, realistic advice and examples of those in the know, the home-based workers themselves. In the process of writing this book, I discovered the ingenuity, determination and motivation behind some of Australia's hardest-working and most successful small businesses. That was for me, and I hope will be for the reader of this book, a fascinating and exhilarating, rewarding and encouraging experience.

All information was accurate at the time of printing. While written in good faith, the publisher and author are not responsible for any adverse consequences arising from the use of any information supplied in this book.

INTRODUCTION

Today's technology gives us choices and options—the choice to select an appropriate and appealing work environment and the option of having a flexible work base. Working from home is the smart career move of the 1990s. As your own boss, you have adjustable work patterns and structure. You can create your work content, meaning and goal, whether that be working solely to obtain sufficient income so as to spend more time with your family or whether that be to combine a home office with headquarters in the city so as to work more efficiently and comfortably.

I am writing this at my desk on a Thursday morning before leaving for my regular game of tennis. The window of my home office overlooks a large front garden in a quiet street, a relaxing outlook. Not for me the dash through heavy traffic, the overbearing boss, the rigid work hours and dreary, time-consuming meetings. I have control and autonomy over my work day and its structure, having exercise and time off when I choose and making up the time in the evening. I am achieving more with less frustration and with more satisfaction.

I feel happier, am more productive and am in charge of my own life and destiny.

Join me. Over 400,000 Australians already have and the numbers are growing daily.

1

A NEW LIFE BECKONS

Because they run their own hydraulics business from their home in Cairns, Charlie and Kaye Ross are able to spend more time with their children. They are always home when the youngsters return from school. For Charlie, who 'lives and breathes hydraulics', being near his work all the time is perfect. 'This is my life and my hobby,' he says. Partners in business and compatible in personality, the Rosses have also reduced stress with this arrangement. 'We have fewer arguments now that we are together,' says Kaye, 'and, with five children ranging in age from seven to eighteen, I would not otherwise be able to work.'

Roger Fountain can head down to the beach at Byron Bay, NSW, and surf in the late afternoon when there is a lull in his work. Yet he never misses out on a business opportunity, being able to respond promptly to interstate or international faxes, whether these arrive at ten at night or seven in the morning. As one of three directors of a company that specialises in the oil seed market—with his co-directors living in Geelong, Victoria, and Brisbane, Queensland—Fountain must always be within easy contact. His mobile telephone and personal computer with modem have become indispensable. Modern technology has allowed him to leave a frenetic life in Sydney, where he used to commute several hours daily, and concentrate on quality of life.

These individuals are part of a growing number of Australians who, from choice or necessity, have joined the global trend towards working from home. They are taking advantage of the freedom and flexibility such employment offers.

They have become part of the 1990s trend—the ever-increasing number of people the world over who have traded jobs in hectic, noisy offices for home-based occupations.

Technological advances and falling prices have put sophisticated equipment within their reach.

They benefit from lower overheads and less travel, coupled with increased income, job satisfaction, personal well-being and motivation. And these people do not run only small cottage-style businesses. Some turnover millions of dollars a year. Employees of big companies who work at home one or two days a week are also happier, more efficient and more productive than those who work full-time in the company office.

So what are you waiting for?

Whether you want to escape from a frenzied lifestyle, office politics and lengthy meetings or simply be your own boss and develop your own product, home-based work can provide you with both the means and the opportunity.

First things first

So—you've decided that working for yourself from home looks like an attractive proposition. First things first. *Can* you do it? Have you got what it takes? Are you suited to such work and to such a lifestyle?

Before you look at *what* you would do, and *how* and *why* you would do it, ask yourself the following vital questions.

Are you suited to working from home?

1. Are you happy working alone or with one other person?
   a. No

b. Sometimes, but I also need social contact
c. Yes

2. Are you a well-organised person?
   a. Reasonably—and I can improve
   b. No, everything's always in a mess
   c. Organisation is my middle name!
3. Do you set yourself realistic goals and work towards them?
   a. Yes, how else can I get anywhere?
   b. Usually
   c. Goals? I'm not playing sport
4. How often do you achieve these goals?
   a. Most of the time
   b. Always
   c. Never
5. Are you prepared to do all the work associated with your business—from marketing to typing and invoicing, from bookkeeping to cleaning?
   a. No
   b. Maybe—or I can hire others to do so
   c. Definitely—when can I start?
6. Does the prospect of being your own boss appeal to you?
   a. Most certainly
   b. No way—who can I blame or turn to when things go wrong?
   c. I'll think about it
7. Are motivation, discipline and persistence part of your make-up?
   a. How did you know?
   b. Perhaps, on good days
   c. My motto is 'Put off today what you can do tomorrow'
8. Do you need to work under constant supervision?
   a. Sometimes, but I'll get used to working for myself
   b. No—but I do appreciate praise and encouragement from my peers
   c. Yes—this is what gives me confidence and self-esteem
9. Does the prospect of working long hours for less money, at least initially, put you off?
   a. No—I have a goal
   b. Possibly—but I'm aware of that from the start and I have drive and ambition

c. More work and less pay? The job I have now is just fine, thank you!

10. Are you easily discouraged? Do you need constant reassurance from others?
    a. No to both—I'm independent and a self-starter
    b. Yes and double yes
    c. At times—but I'm seeking a new challenge

Check your scores

1. a) 1 b) 2 c) 3
2. a) 2 b) 1 c) 3
3. a) 3 b) 2 c) 1
4. a) 2 b) 3 c) 1
5. a) 1 b) 2 c) 3
6. a) 3 b) 1 c) 2
7. a) 3 b) 2 c) 1
8. a) 2 b) 3 c) 1
9. a) 3 b) 2 c) 1
10. a) 3 b) 1 c) 2

A score between 21 and 30
What are you waiting for? You have the aptitude and the motivation to work for yourself from home. Read on and learn how to do it.

A score between 11 and 20
You're considering the possibility. You're weighing the advantages against the disadvantages. You're not totally committed but you're open to the prospect. Read on and learn more.

A score between 1 and 10
So what's wrong with your present job or situation? You're not the ideal person to be working from home—yet.

But don't give up on the idea. Jim Penman once did a business magazine quiz called 'Have you the makings of an entrepreneur?' He bombed out completely, with such a low score that he was advised to stick to his safe and secure job. His response was a hearty laugh. At the time, *Business Review Weekly* had named his business, Jim's Mowing, which Penman had started from his home, one of Australia's fastest-growing businesses, with 210 lawnmowing franchisees to its credit! So take heart, read on, and discover how others have succeeded.

The quiz and list is merely a guide. Skills can be learnt. Even your personality and character can be modified, although this can take a little longer. But if you're motivated, informed and realistic about your expectations, and above all if you're determined to succeed, great things can be achieved. In the words of US President Calvin Coolidge:

> Nothing in the world can take the place of persistence.
> Talent will not; nothing is more common than unsuccessful men with talent.
> Education will not; the world is full of educated derelicts.
> Genius will not; unrewarded genius is almost a proverb.
> Persistence and determination alone are omnipotent.
> The slogan 'press on' has solved and always will solve the problems of the human race.

Perhaps you prefer the philosophy of Bette Midler, who claims, 'You don't need to be smart, good-looking or fantastic. All you need is to be enthusiastic!'

Facts and figures

It has been estimated that some 400,000 Australians, at least 4 per cent of the workforce, presently work from home-based offices making use of the latest computer, fax and telephone technology. And according to Adrian Lynch of the Asia Pacific Telework Association, this figure is growing by 15 to 17 per cent annually. Reflecting the size of the trend, he says, is the fact that 'The biggest sales of personal computers in 1995 and 1996 were to home offices, not big companies.'

Telstra predicts that, thanks to rapid advances in technology, one in every four Australians will be working from home within the next ten years. It says this will deliver employers productivity gains worth $1 billion and save the community $500 million as a result of reduced traffic congestion, noise and pollution.

The latest Australian Bureau of Statistics publication on the topic is 'Persons Employed at Home, September 1995'. This survey, which excludes farmers, farmhands and farm assistants, defines a person employed at home as *someone who works more hours at home than elsewhere.* Its total of 343,300 such persons represents an increase of 11.5 per cent over the last

Figure 1 Percentage of Australians with a Personal Computer ('PC')/ Answering Machine ('AM')/Mobile Phone/Fax at Home 1991 to 1996

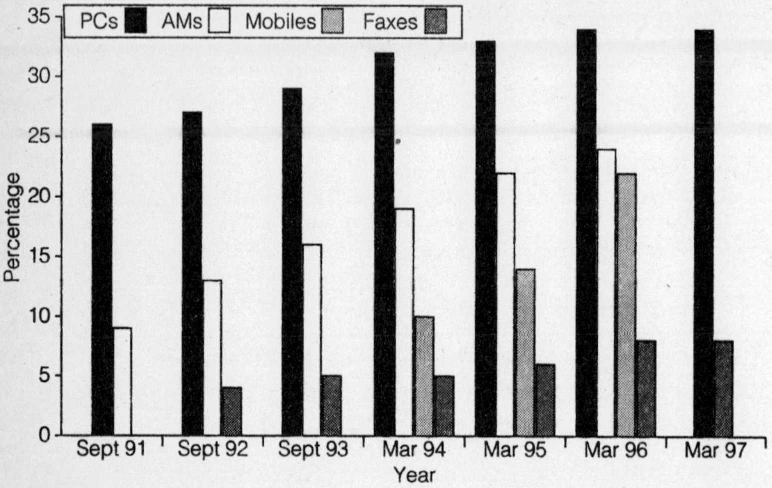

survey in March 1992, but does not exclude those who work both at home and at another location. The report on the September 1995 survey did note, though, that 2.1 million people, or 26 per cent of Australia's labour force, worked some hours each week at home. Here are its main findings:

Numbers—how many Australians work from home?

- An estimated 8.3 million persons aged fifteen and over were employed in September 1995. Of these, 26 per cent worked some hours at home while 4 per cent were employed at home.

Self-employment—being your own boss

- More than half of those employed at home (52 per cent) worked for themselves, being 'own account workers or contributing family workers', while 37 per cent were employees.

Age—how old are these home-based workers?

- People in older age groups were more likely to be

Figure 2 Growth in percentage of Australians with a PC, Fax Machine, Mobile Phone or Answering Machine at Home—1991 to 1996

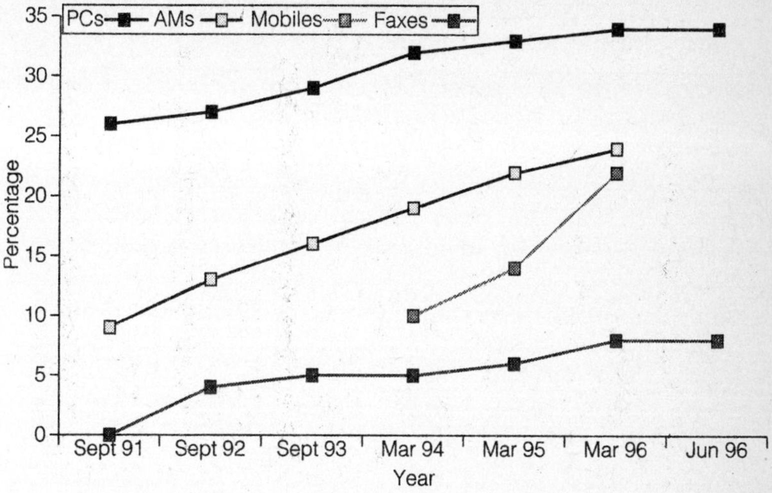

Note: The latest research, undertaken by Keig and Company up until the end of 1996, has discovered that personal computers are now found in 56 per cent of Australian homes. This figure is expected to rise to 66 per cent in the next two years.

employed at home than younger persons. Just over 1 per cent of those aged 15 to 24 were employed at home. Five per cent of 35- to 44–year-olds were employed at home. This proportion rises to 8 per cent for those aged 55 and over.

Male and female—who is more likely to work from home?

- The number of women employed at home (230,700) was more than double the number of men employed at home (112,600). Women employed at home made up 6.4 per cent of all employed females. Men employed at home comprised 2.4 per cent of all employed males.

Reasons for working at home—why do it?

- The most commonly given reason for starting work at home was 'to open/operate own/family business (with spouse)'.

This was the reason given by 27 per cent of persons working at home; 18 per cent gave the reason as 'wanted office at home/no overheads/no rent'; and 17 per cent said 'children too young/preferred to look after children'. Of those employed at home who were married, 54 per cent had children below the age of 15.

Occupation—what are these home-based workers doing?

- Most of those working at home were clerks (39 per cent), the great majority being women (95 per cent). More men than women were employed at home as managers and administrators, professionals, para-professionals and tradespersons. Those industries with the highest numbers of persons employed at home were property and business services (20 per cent) and construction (14.6 per cent).

Hours worked—how long are they putting in?

- Almost two-thirds of those employed at home usually worked fewer than 35 hours a week at home. An estimated 28 per cent worked 40 hours or more. Some 49 per cent of males employed at home worked 40 hours or more compared with 18 per cent of females.

Qualifications—how educated are they?

- The March 1992 survey found that more than half of self-employed persons working at home (56 per cent) had post-school qualifications. More men than women had post-school qualifications: 67 per cent compared with 49 per cent.

Duration of self-employment—for how long have they been home-based?

- As at September 1995, 55 per cent of self-employed persons working at home had been doing so for less than five years and 9 per cent had been working at home for 20 years or longer.

The Roy Morgan Research Centre has found that the numbers of personal computers, answering machines, fax machines, and mobile phones in homes are increasing steadily. Its June 1996 survey discovered that 53 per cent of Australians now have at least one of these four items in their home.

Looking at the products more likely to be connected with a home office, it found that 8 per cent of those surveyed had a fax machine at home, 34 per cent had a computer, 6 per cent a modem, and 14 per cent had software for business purposes.

So—what can I do at home?

There are different degrees and various ways of running a home-based business. There are trades and occupations that you always knew were home-based and others that will surprise you. The only limitations are:

- whether your business is appropriate to a home location;
- whether your business can get local or council approval to operate;

and, naturally, home-based or not:

- whether your business is a viable option.

If the answer to all three is 'yes', then the only other limit is your imagination!

So *what* do people offer in a home-based business? One of three things.

They:

- provide a service;
- sell a product;
- manufacture a product.

Providing a service can range from typing to window cleaning, from management consultancy to graphic design or dental treatment.

Selling can be by means of direct retail or wholesale. It can be over the telephone (telemarketing), door to door (as with Avon), party plan (as with Tupperware) or network or multi-level marketing (as with Amway). You can grow and sell herbs or flowers or raise snails for gourmet palates.

As for *manufacture*, you can make wetsuits or fashion outfits, sew mosquito nets or create wonderful jewellery.

One point to bear in mind, however, is that not all of these enterprises will be classified as home-based businesses.

If you sell some $1000 worth of Avon or Amway products each year, for example, you are not technically operating a business and you will not be eligible for the corresponding tax deductions. On the other hand, should you be making $60,000 a year with a mobile telephone and fax machine to handle your cosmetic orders, you most certainly are running a business. And a very successful one at that!

This topic will be covered in detail in Chapter 5, 'Money Matters'.

So how do I work from home?

The flexibility and versatility of home-based work are endless. Some people merely use their home as a base, as an electrician or plumber may do. Others do their work entirely at home—painting ceramics or operating a medical, accounting or legal practice. Some use their home-based occupation only to supplement their partner's earnings. Some work from home on a tentative basis, establishing whether their business can provide them with a living or waiting until it has grown sufficiently to move out into rented premises. This is how electrical appliance giant Kambrook started.

Nowadays many home workers make extensive use of computer and telecommunications technology. Some, known as telecommuters, put in a few days at the office and work remotely from home the rest of the week. And others again are full-time teleworkers—self-employed and servicing a number of clients from home.

Teleworking

Professor Jack Wood introduced the idea of teleworking and telecommuting to Australia almost ten years ago. The concept was originally created in the late 1960s by American Professor Jack Nilles who, in conversation with a city-planner, realised that the problem of commuter traffic could be solved in one easy move—by people working at home! He developed this theme at the University of Southern California and coined the term 'telecommuting' by combining the words, and the meaning of the words—'telecommunications' and 'commuting'.

Professor Jack Wood, known as the Father of Telecommuting in Australia, just as Professor Jack Nilles is in America, describes a telecommuter as someone who works from home for a main employer part-time, and at the head office for the rest of the time. He or she is able to link in with the head office by means of computer technology.

A home base allows you to continue working in your full-time job, for an employer such as the Public Service, and be located at home for part of your week. A pilot program run by the New South Wales Roads and Traffic Authority gave telecommuting a trial in 1994. For six months, 77 surveyors, systems officers, clerks, engineers and computer systems officers spent one or two days at home and the rest of the week in the main office. The results were positive: productivity rose and employees reported they felt happier and less stressed with this arrangement. One found that what took her half a day to do in the office took an hour at home!

According to Paul Chung, former national manager for telecommuting and home business at Telstra, telecommuting is also good for companies because it 'opens up huge possibilities of improving customer service'. Companies that can call on a pool of tele-linked home workers can offer 24-hour service or rapidly reorganise work shifts without worrying about getting workers to and from head office.

Teleworking can give individuals enormous freedom. Chung knows of a computer scientist who lives in Ballina, NSW, yet holds down a job in California via telecommunications links.

There is also the ever-increasing phenomenon known as outsourcing, whereby large companies and organisations recruit an individual for a project on a contract basis. This can prove cheaper and more efficient for the company in the long run. The contract worker does not have holiday or sick pay but the salary is slightly higher in order to compensate for this. Better work may be obtained from the outsource worker, eager to build up a reputation and hence obtain regular work. In this way, such an arrangement can suit both parties.

You may be able to work for a large company in the convenience of your own home. When Paul Chung rang his travel agent to organise a flight from Sydney to Brisbane, he discovered the person with whom he spoke was based at her home. 'This opens up huge possibilities of improving customer service,' he says. 'Telecommuting changes the whole structure of work.'

Roger Fountain has even more freedom thanks to his mobile office, a laptop, fax modem and mobile phone that fit in a briefcase and let him work from a Sydney hotel one day and a Perth apartment the next. Says Chung: 'with technology, we can now distribute work and people can live the way they like. We can release the constraints that have been put upon us by industrialisation. Where management was once by control and a rigid hierarchical structure, it can now be run on trust and results.'

Yet whether your set-up is basic or state-of-the-art, you'll still need to make it work to your best advantage. Here's how.

Where to start

In making the move to a home business, most people rely on the skills, background and experience they already have. But some, like former builder John Ehm of Cairns, strike out in radical new directions. Ehm set up Homechain, a home accommodation service for tourists. But since he had no previous knowledge or involvement in tourism, he was careful to do extensive research first, spending almost eight months investigating the market and talking to industry bodies and local government.

Adelaide graphic artist Kym Duval took the more usual course of moving from employment in a company to doing the same work in his own home-based business. 'I wanted to be the master of my own destiny and, after working for others for sixteen years, I knew what was involved,' he says.

Be aware of the risks and the drawbacks

Whichever route you choose, though, remember the Boy Scout motto: 'Be prepared'. *Ninety per cent of small businesses fail within a decade.* And *11 per cent fail in the first three months,* according to Professor Alan Williams, formerly Professor of Management at the University of Newcastle. His research over

20 years found that in all parts of Australia, on average, 30 per cent of small businesses fail in the first year and 68 to 70 per cent by the end of the fifth year. There is, he points out, a wide variation between industries in their failure rates. Consulting engineers, for example, have a lower failure rate, per capita, than used-car salespeople.

Do bear in mind that these figures apply to *all* small businesses and not specifically home-based ones. We will consider why such businesses fail in Chapter 2, but the main thing to be aware of is that just being good at mowing lawns, selling gourmet jams or making snazzy business suits is not enough. Once you're in your own business, you are responsible for *all* aspects of that business. Its success or failure is on *your* shoulders.

Advantages of working from home

Independence and total control

'Working for myself from home has given me enjoyment and opportunity I would not have otherwise had,' says Brisbane real estate investment guru Jan Somers, a former high school teacher whose first self-published book *Building Wealth through Investment Property* has sold more than 200,000 copies. A millionaire who retired from teaching at 37, Somers is now on a mission to show others the way to financial independence.

Flexibility and versatility

'I can bend my working hours around other commitments and still get the same amount of work done in a day,' explains Sue Carney, a senior editor at Reader's Digest who works from her Blue Mountains home three days a week and travels to the Sydney office on other days. 'If I was in the office, I might have to take half a day off work in order to take the children to a dental appointment. This way, I can make up that lost time in the evening once the children are asleep.'

Cairns desktop publisher Mil Clay lights the outdoor barbecue for the family, returns to work in his office for a short while and then joins them to cook the steak.

You want to play golf on Wednesday afternoons? Do it. You'd like to play tennis each morning or go to the gym three times a week? Go right ahead. Take Friday off for a drive into the hills and work on Sunday instead. Do what you want, what suits *you*.

Job creation and increased work opportunities

'I looked everywhere for employment and I was prepared to do anything, even sweep the roads,' says 61-year-old Roy Williams, who spent almost four years looking for work when he arrived in Australia from England. 'People thought I was too old. So I started a home business in my old trade—manufacturing wetsuits—and I haven't looked back since.' In fact, Roy has been swamped with orders!

If your situation does not permit office-based work—perhaps you are in a wheelchair with no transport available, housebound due to children, or other reasons—you can still work from home.

Working from home allows you to start up an entirely new business or specialise in one line of your present work.

Nelli Greer custom-makes mosquito nets from her Cairns home. 'I was forced into starting my own business and initially worked from home to cut costs,' she says. 'Mind you, I'm not complaining. Being at home means I am always here for my daughter, and where else can you have a balcony workplace surrounded by luscious rainforest?'

Time and money saved in travel

'I save on commuting hours and so avoid considerable stress and strain,' says organisational psychologist Bruce Crowe, who lives and works on the tenth floor of a Sydney mixed residential and commercial apartment building. 'I go out one door, walk one metre and enter another door to my home office.'

More time to spend with family

'I am able to watch my sons grow up, and that's a priceless experience,' says Adelaide building designer Elvio Ferrara. 'I can pick up young Michael from school, and when my clients see my children, it breaks down the formality and softens the image.'

Cost savings

'I save at least $25,000 a year in rent,' says Cairns author, cartoonist and speaker Andrew Matthews. 'That's enabled me to buy a tennis court—vital in my case. I love the sport and aim to play daily.'

Potential for a higher income

'My wages now depend on the amount of effort I put in,' says computer consultant and reseller Wesley Brown. 'That's a great incentive. I like the fact that my income is driven by my capabilities and by what I've produced. If I didn't have to sleep, I'd be making a fortune!'

'My home business grew enough to provide two incomes, so my husband joined me,' says Jan Sutherland of Dial-A-Wife Cleaning Services. 'We are now expanding into an agency situation. We presently employ 25 to 30 people.'

Increased productivity and job satisfaction

This is due to fewer interruptions and distractions. Your noisy office has now become a peaceful environment, conducive to good work. 'I am much happier and more fulfilled working at home on my own. Now I can continue to aim at achieving the impossible with less disturbances,' laughs Jenny Church of Your Type Secretarial.

Drawbacks of working from home

Isolation

Without other people to gossip with and bounce off, some home workers feel lonely and isolated. Once the initial burst of enthusiasm has waned, you may start losing touch with your colleagues and with changes in your profession. With no pressure from boss or workmates, you may realise your dedication and persistence are sadly lacking. Your motivation slips, you find yourself getting up later and later—and producing less and less.

Loneliness

You haven't seen any of your friends for days. They seem to have forgotten you exist. The invitations are no longer flooding in. You would even welcome a distracting telephone call or coffee break with an acquaintance.

'I'm always alone in my work. I would prefer to have others around me,' declares jewellery manufacturer and porcelain artist Beate Wickert. Together with her architect husband, she moved from a large Sydney warehouse, where she worked with others, to a large home on the outskirts of Cairns. A warmer climate, an outdoor and more tranquil lifestyle have been benefits of the move that help to offset the isolation. And, with agents for her work in New South Wales and Victoria, Wickert's talents are not limited to Queensland.

Irregular income

You also have to get used to an *irregular income*. 'I'll have nothing for some time and then all the money will come through at once,' says interior designer Anna Pyrzakowski. 'That can be a problem at the time. But by the end of the year, it will have averaged out to a decent salary.'

Work is always there

And there's no *escape from work*. It's always there. Your partner complains: 'You are always working—evenings, weekends, it never stops. You are putting in *more* hours than at the office and yet you're earning *less*. What's the point?'

You start to feel you've escaped from work only to be trapped at home looking at the same four walls. And you can't afford to go away. 'If I take longer than a week's holiday, the work builds up too much,' says Keith Bainbridge, who runs a credit control service. 'You need to plan holidays and juggle them with the workflow, a few days' break here and there throughout the year.'

Not taken seriously by family, friends and neighbours

Some people seem to think that, because you are based at home, *you are available* all the time. Partners may expect extra help around the house, friends may demand long lunches and neighbours may drop in for lengthy cups of coffee. 'My husband would refer to the time I "gave up work" and, when leaving home for his job, would ask me to vacuum this or dust that when I had a moment,' says Adelaide gourmet food products manufacturer Philippa Kerslake. Having left a long-time career in the corporate world because of growing disillusionment—'there is no equal opportunity in the way women are treated'—she found she had to start all over by re-educating her husband about her new occupation.

Professional image

Some home workers have to struggle with *clients' perception that a home-based business is less professional* than one based in a commercial office. 'While I don't hide the fact I work from home, I don't publicise it either,' says Anna Pyrzakowski, who fears that if she does say she has a home office, she may lose work to larger inner-city companies.

Insufficient work

And what happens when the *work is intermittent* or insufficient? 'The number of clients fluctuates,' says Adelaide homoeopath Meredith Norman. 'In addition to that, I am generous with my time and found it hard initially to ask for money.' Though she set up the home base for financial reasons—'I wanted to reduce the [total] costs of rent'—Meredith has had to learn to stick to her stipulated fees.

Distractions

Then there are the *distractions*. 'The problems for me at home are the fridge, the TV and the telephone,' says Adelaide writer Peter Goldsworthy. 'And, since I've got onto the Internet, I am using any excuse to surf it. I know of other writers who have had to rent out an office in order to overcome distractions.'

Fear of failure

You're on your own now—which is fine when things are going well. But you can't help *fearing failure*. What about when there's a downturn? When will you be paid? *Will* you be paid? That big payment you were expecting is a week overdue. Without it, you can't pay *your* bills. What will happen? The gas and electricity will be cut off, the telephone will be disconnected, your car and house will be repossessed . . . Before you know it, one unpaid account has escalated—in your mind at least—into a catastrophe.

Lack of promotion opportunities

The saying '*out of sight, out of mind*' can be very true when you work from home. 'If you are working for an organisation from your home base, you still need to regularly go into the head office and keep in touch with your colleagues,' says Paul Chung. Otherwise, 'You can be forgotten or overlooked when it comes to promotion and you can easily lose touch with office politics and developments.' You may lose status and self-esteem as well. 'My neighbours noticed that I spent a lot of time at home. They asked me whether I had lost my job or been made redundant,' laughs Chung.

Now, read on

If, having assessed your personal skills and considered both pluses and minuses, you think working from home will be your cup of tea, this book is here to help. You will learn how to get started, what rules and regulations govern your proposed business and how to set up your home office in practical, straightforward steps. You will also discover how to create a welcoming work environment, tailored to your unique needs, on a reasonable budget. And while on the subject of money, it is vital to organise your finances and fees correctly from the outset. Chapter 4 tackles this topic in detail.

Your Home Business will teach you how to present your business professionally with flair and style and give it that competitive edge. Case histories and examples of home-based businesses sprinkled throughout the text present you with many years of accumulated business experience and knowledge, providing valuable insights and advice relevant to *your* home-based venture. Learn how Peter Goldsworthy deals with the solitude of writing, how dietitian and nutritionist Rosemary Stanton handles lunchtimes and what real estate guru Jan Somers recommends for alleviating work tension.

From designing an effective business card to selecting your home office furniture, or from promoting your business to learning how to deal with the overwhelming response it generates, this book will cover every aspect of your new, fulfilling and ultimately highly successful business life. With careful planning and preparation, you will come to value the fact that home is where the work is!

Exercise

Put aside half an hour and write down the pluses and minuses of your working from home. Leave this for a few days—go back and revise it. By all means, talk with your family, friends and colleagues. But listen to what they say with caution. Have any of them ever contemplated working from home? Are they risk-takers or tentative types?

'Working from home is too risky,' some people will tell you. 'Why chuck in a perfectly secure job? Anyway, what about your long service leave?'

Your long service leave? Your heart sinks. Your long service leave is not due for another two years! How can you hang on that long?

That's when a new life beckons.

THE STUFF OF DREAMS

Cabinet-maker Brian McNulty is typical of many home-based workers. 'I have rarely worked for a boss,' he says. 'I've never been one to take orders, I prefer to get on and do things my own way. I am ambitious, have a lot of drive and am self-disciplined above all else. If it takes seven days a week to finish the job, I'll do it.'

Personality plays a big part in the success of a home-based business. With no one watching over or guiding you, with no building full of work colleagues inspiring or spurring you on, motivation must come from within. For some, this is the ideal situation. With the freedom that comes from running their own business, these individuals excel.

'I have never had a day when I have not wanted to go to work,' Brian enthuses. 'I've found I have a far more imaginative approach to my trade when working for myself.' After serving his apprenticeship for an old and well-established Melbourne company, Berkowitz and Sons, McNulty developed his skills by working there for several years. 'This was in the 1950s and I was given a lot of free rein, working under my own direction. I did one-off work, high-class antique reproductions—dining settings, bed-room furniture, coffee tables—the stuff you dream about.'

He left to travel around Australia with his wife, before settling in Sydney and working in several partnerships. The McNultys now live in Bundanoon, in NSW, where Brian runs his own home-based business.

'At one stage, I was spending almost four hours a day driving from one side of Sydney to another in peak-hour traffic,' he says. 'I hated that. Today I live halfway between Sydney and Canberra, in a farmhouse on five acres of beautiful country. We have a dirt road, tank water, no postal delivery and we couldn't be happier. This is the prettiest part of New South Wales and the lifestyle is very relaxed.'

Brian gutted the stables on his property, painting them white and installing windows for extra light, to create his workshop. He is there from 7 a.m. most days, busy with his orders. 'I can easily spend weeks or even months on a single item, such as the copy of a Chippendale pedestal desk on which I'm presently working,' says Brian. This faithful copy of an original, with mahogany groundwork overlaid with French walnut, will cost the customer many thousands of dollars.

'I survive because there is no way in the world you can go to a manufacturer set up to produce quantity and get a fine-quality one-off item. To be successful, you need to be in a niche market. You have to specialise or else bigger concerns will eat you alive on cost,' Brian advises. 'It is a very competitive field and you have to know what you are doing. If you are starting off making kitchens, for example, and you don't have the latest computer-controlled equipment, you will have to work that much harder to make your business a success.

'I see a lot of young fellas with a dream. But they all want to start off where I'm finishing. I can understand this "now" generation, but you really need patience.'

Ironically, Brian was pushed into his present position. 'The State Bank of New South Wales foreclosed on my business in 1991, as it did on thousands of others who also went broke overnight. I was thirteen months away from paying off a fourteen-year loan for my factory premises. All my liquid assets were taken, so my business could not continue. I still had all my woodworking machinery and so I moved to Bundanoon. Now I visit Sydney every three weeks or so and I am far happier. This suits me fine. I use my fax machine to transmit drawings and quotes and do the rest of my business over the phone.'

At 60-plus, McNulty says he is past the empire-building stage and has all he wants—'a reasonable income, good quality of life and time with the family'.

For those starting out in a home business, he stresses the importance of preparation. 'You have to plan ahead. You need imagination and you need coping skills. I bought some of my equipment second-hand and made other pieces myself. I upgraded a bit at a time.'

'You need to be aware that there will be a lot of work time for which you will not get paid, time spent in finding work.'

'One of the downsides of working from home is that you cannot produce nothing and expect to survive, and you need to be prepared to work the extra hours. The bottom line is that, if you're working for yourself, you've got to be prepared. You need to be very self-disciplined.

'Mind you, if I had my time over, I would do exactly the same. This is magic.'

TOURISM FROM HOME

When John Ehm decided to go into business in Cairns, he carefully considered his interests as well as his experience and actually gave more weight to the former—a decision with which some would disagree.

'I looked for a business that gave me a mix of the things I wanted to do when I retired,' John explained. 'I wanted to use my talents, to travel widely and visit cattle stations and properties. I was looking for both enjoyment and work.'

His idea was a tourist venture. 'Our family had done some hosting for Expo '88 when we lived in Brisbane. Visitors from Western Australia, Victoria and South Australia stayed with us, and we provided them with breakfast and the evening meal. They would go to Expo during the day, and in the evenings we would talk with them and share experiences.'

When he lost a contract job a few years later and moved to Cairns, John started thinking about a home accommodation business for tourists. 'I asked a few people in the tourist industry what they thought and then I placed a few advertisements in the local paper to ask whether families were interested in joining such a network organisation.'

To his delight, John received more than 60 replies from the north Queensland area, offering a range of accommodation styles from suburban homes to farms and outback stations. Greatly encouraged, he suggested to his wife, Emmy, that they consider starting up such a business.

'It is my nature to research before I do things, so I spent almost eight months in investigation, talking to industry bodies and local government,' says John. He wanted to find out whether his concept would be a viable business proposition. 'It is a small niche market but my research, in 1992, showed there was a strong trend developing. People are venturing away from the major tourist destinations and penetrating into the real Australia, and the perfect place to do this is in homes. Here they can meet people, talk about what life is like in Australia and interact on a friendship level, quite unlike the situation in a motel.'

Although John had had many years of self-employment as a builder, he decided to polish up his skills by attending a 21-hour small business course at the local TAFE college. That led him to apply to SEVS, the Self-Employed Venture Scheme, a Queensland government initiative. Similar schemes exist in other states, under different names.

'SEVS provides financial assistance—an interest-free loan—to start a business,' says John. 'To get it I needed a business plan, so I put together a comprehensive proposal, which was approved.' John then had to attend a three-week small business management course. 'This complemented the other course I had done,' he says.

John and Emmy decided to start up their business from home. 'Although I had included the cost of renting an office in my business plan, I decided a home office would give us breathing space in case the business did not fulfil expectations. We could pull out easily and would not be tied to any lease.' They sought council approval for this. Neighbours were made aware of John's intention and asked to register any complaints they might have. There were none and so, a few weeks later, Homechain was in business.

John's groundwork had told him that Cairns is one of the top 20 holiday destinations in the world. Whereas the bulk of tourists visiting states such as South Australia were domestic, most of those visiting Queensland—and Cairns in particular—were from overseas. This knowledge prompted John to advertise Homechain in Britain and Germany as well as on the Australian Tourist Commission's overseas database.

Four years later, 'The business has exceeded our expectations,' John says happily. 'We have joined the Aussie Host movement, which has established our credentials and gained us a reputation. And having a home-office environment has proved to be very appropriate and a real advantage for us.'

Before starting his business, John worked up to it in a logical and methodical manner. First he decided what business he would take on. Then he researched its viability and the rules and regulations that would apply. He gained the necessary business skills by attending relevant courses, and obtained the requisite permissions from local or state government. While all this was no guarantee that he would succeed, by preparing himself and making himself knowledgeable about the market, he minimised the risks.

2

GETTING STARTED

There are no certainties in life and there are many spectacular examples of highly researched products and businesses that have failed dismally. Conversely, others have boomed despite their owners' lack of a business plan or any great preparation or forethought.

Jim's Mowing, now the largest lawnmowing franchise in the world, with over 1,000 franchisees, was started with a $24 investment, from home, by a man who freely admits he is, by nature, a total slob with little natural business talent.

'I am the most disorganised person and I have made hideous mistakes,' says Jim Penman. His business and others like it may owe their success to a combination of skills, persistence and motivation in other areas. Or just to their owners' being in the right place at the right time. Whatever the case, such success stories are the exception rather than the rule.

Better to bear in mind the saying, 'If you fail to plan, then you plan to fail'.

Before you start your business, it is wise to prepare thoroughly. Here's a step-by-step guide.

GETTING STARTED CHECKLIST

1. *What sort of business is for you?*
   Consider your qualifications, experience, talents, skills and expertise and interests.
2. *Is your business viable?*
   - Is there a market for your proposed business?
   - Is that market large enough to provide the income you want?
   - Who are your competitors, or are you creating a new market?
   - Do you have suitable premises?
   - Is a shopfront necessary for your business?
   - Can your business be legally run from home?
   - What are your local council regulations regarding home-based work?
   - Do you have sufficient start-up and reserve capital?
   - Do you have adequate business skills and knowledge, and if not, can you get them?
   - Are there professionals—bank manager, solicitor, accountant, local business centre—that can advise you?
3. *How will you operate?*
   - Will you work part-time or full-time?
   - Will you ease into a home business while still keeping your present job?
   - Is this a permanent arrangement or will you test the market before renting other premises?
   - What will your business status be—sole trader, partnership, or limited liability company?
   - What will your business name be?
   - Will you start a new business or buy an existing business?
   - Will you buy into and operate as a franchise?
   - What hours will you work?

What sort of business is for you?

Some people find their professional *qualifications* are well suited to a home business. After obtaining the degree of

Bachelor of Dental Surgery from the University of Adelaide and working in a partnership for many years, Derick Thomas decided to start up his own dental practice from home. It has been a successful move for him. 'I feel completely in control here, in my own kingdom,' he says. 'My previous location was insecure—subject to leases and changes in ownership of the building.'

Other people have qualifications but choose *not* to make use of them. Ross Sutherland had had enough of teaching so he took a redundancy package and joined his wife Jan in her Dial-A-Wife cleaning service. 'I loved the teaching and the children, and I had worked at the same school for thirteen years,' he says, 'but the politics in recent years had got me down.'

Experience counts for a great deal too. If you have had many years of experience in the fashion retail industry, you might decide to make clothes at home and sell them yourself. The added advantage of this, as opposed to starting up a business from scratch, is that you know the industry well and have the contacts. Your previous employers may not be too happy to find that you are now a competitor, but there are ways around this. Why not work with them, perhaps even supply them?

Geelong architect Wayne Ketchen does contract work for major companies in Melbourne, including the one for which he used to work. 'I lost my job because of the recession, so it was not my decision to leave,' he says. 'Still, I would have gone out on my own at some stage. This just speeded up the process. I literally finished one job on Friday and started my own business on Monday. Now I work for private clients and companies, and my last employer still supplies me with work.' If you can maintain a good relationship with your previous employer, this can be advantageous to both parties.

Denis Carroll believes his South Australian food wholesale business is successful because of his background. 'I have good extensive training in the area, having worked for national manufacturers,' he says. 'Although my business is not yet paying me a huge income, I do not believe it would have worked at all without a knowledge of the marketplace. A public servant with no such experience, taking a redundancy package, could not have done this.'

If you haven't got suitable qualifications or experience, you might put your personal *talents* to work. You may be a fabulous piano player or a gourmet cook. Have you thought of giving music lessons or establishing a home catering business? 'I've always loved music, right from childhood,' says Hazel Matters, of Adelaide. When she retired from schoolteaching in 1992, she decided to instruct students in piano and singing at home. Now she indulges in her passion while making a part-time income. Doing something you truly enjoy for a living can be an added bonus.

If you have a particular interest, such as birdwatching, gardening or computers, you might find opportunities to write articles for newspapers and magazines. Many such pieces are written by specialists or *aficionados*, rather than journalists. Or you might pass on what you know to others. Many adult education colleges employ individuals able to offer weekly lessons or one-day seminars on a particular subject. While you do not need to be a qualified teacher or lecturer to do this, you must have expert knowledge.

Kay Hannaford started up a lucrative business offering guided walking tours in the Adelaide suburbs. 'I hit upon the idea when I was walking through the city to my government job early one morning,' she says. 'I was pleasantly surprised to discover how popular the concept was.' After running the business for several years, she sold it.

Kay loves meeting and talking to people, so she enjoyed her walking tours. But if dealing with the public reduces you to a gibbering wreck, you might be better off staying put at home.

Peter Goldsworthy, a writer and GP, has found a happy medium between company and solitude: he writes at home in the mornings and works at his wife's medical practice in the afternoons. He spent two years writing full-time, but found that made him lonely and morose. Peter says, 'I can identify with the words of Spanish film director Luis Buñuel: "Solitude is a wonderful thing—so long as you can talk about it with someone afterwards." Having contact with people is very important to me as a writer—it gives me ideas and keeps me grounded. Otherwise I would get too cerebral.'

It's vital, before you set up your home business, to consider whether it will suit your *personality*. 'Looking back to why I left a job in a city office,' says Adelaide computer consultant and reseller Wesley Brown, 'I finally decided I had had enough of being regimented—of getting up at the same time each day and returning home at the same time. I find it very difficult to work for a boss. I like to work on my own, for myself. I am just that sort of person, that sort of personality. Motivation is no problem, I can work for days on end without a break. My income is related to the amount of effort I put in and I think that's great.'

Your personality also includes your body clock. Are you an early riser or do you prefer to work well into the night? What time of day is most productive for you—morning, afternoon or evening? 'I'm an early riser but, working from home, I can also work into the evening,' says Wesley. 'I have flexibility of hours at home.'

Adelaide building designer Elvio Ferrara works until early afternoon and then enjoys a siesta period—cooking the main meal of the day for himself, going to the bank or post office, spending time with the family, sometimes napping—before resuming work in the evening and continuing until 1 a.m. 'The most valuable part of my work day is from 9 p.m. until one,' he says. 'That is uninterrupted work time. The body is most tired in the afternoon, so that is when I take it easy, shop and have the most important meal of the day. I think it is important to have more than a sandwich for lunch. I'll have something light for tea with the family.'

Working into the night can reap big rewards for your business—if you need to communicate across international time zones. Melbourne-based Warwick Rodden, who has a home-based business providing translation services, can keep in regular contact with clients in Seattle, London and Berlin by being available early in the morning or late in the evening.

Is your business viable?

A viable business is one that produces sufficient profits and cash flow. In deciding whether your proposed business is viable, you need to consider the following.

Without a *market* for your goods or services, your business is lost before it even gets off the ground. To assess the size of the market, you'll need to be clear on the range of your business. Do you intend to start—and remain—local or will you be going national or even international? Naturally, this may change: you may expand as demand increases or reduce operations as demand declines. A word of caution: one common reason for small business failure is premature expansion. Suppose you decide to operate solely on a local level. You can now check local newspapers, community noticeboards, shop windows and club newsletters for others offering similar services. Are there already advertisements for your type of business in the *Yellow Pages*? If so, does this simply indicate that there is a demand for such a service, or does it suggest that demand is being adequately met? It is up to you to investigate further here and discover which is the case. Your local small business centre may be able to advise on this. Or you might even talk to your prospective competitors.

If you intend to set up a lawnmowing business in your suburb and find it is already well served by another company, you might extend the services you offer, perhaps doing rubbish removal, tree pruning or weeding—things the other company does not offer.

If you find that a similar type of business has existed in your area but failed, do not give up automatically. *Why* did it fail? Were its prices too high? Were its goods or services poor? Was the business unreliable?

A customer profile can be very useful indeed. If your clientele is going to consist of fashion conscious twenty-somethings, it would be foolish to set up your custom-made clothing business in an area inhabited by retirees.

You can initiate your own market research—doorknocking, placing questionnaires in letterboxes and asking neighbours and local businesses whether they would be interested in your services.

When looking at national and international markets, similar principles apply.

Once you've established the existence and size of the market, you'll need to figure out whether it can provide *the income you want* and, if not, whether you're in business for money or for love. Marilyn Jolly did not go into her home business expecting it to support her financially. And, as it turned out, it doesn't: she's ended up working for pleasure rather than for pay.

Marilyn got the idea for Jolly Home and Pet Care after her own bad experiences. 'My husband and I have a dog, which we put in kennels when we went on holiday,' she says. 'We returned three days later to find her very distressed—she had not been let out of the cage in all that time. Next time round, I asked a friend to house-sit for us. She was to feed and look after the animal, care for the garden and water the plants.' That arrangement proved even more disastrous. 'We came home to find the pot plants dead and the dog missing. So I decided to set up a business minding people's animals and their homes when they are away.'

Keen to make her service accessible, Marilyn actually undercharges. 'I had to charge less than the kennels in order to get business. When I look at the time and travel involved, I realise I am doing this for love rather than money.' She charges just $12 a day to check on the house, walk the dog for 30 minutes and clear the garden of droppings, take in the mail, put out the rubbish, water the plants and attend to any other chores the owner has requested. She advertises in three local papers and wishes she had a bigger budget—to extend to television and radio. Yet she is reluctant to charge more, as she believes people cannot afford to pay any more. So her market is limited to local suburbs—a drive of more than 30 minutes would make the whole venture unviable. Nor can she afford to hire help at busy times: she herself cannot make a reliable living.

Will your business need a *shopfront* to attract customers? If so, think again. Only retail outlets in commercial areas are allowed to have shopfronts, not home-based businesses in residential zones. You may be able to make or repair shoes at home, but you will not be able to have a window displaying your work. Advertising will have to be done by other means. Regulations regarding signs vary from state to state. In South Australia, for example, you are permitted to display one sign, so long as it is no larger than 20 cm square and is placed on your property, on the fence or the door, and not on the street. Check with your local council.

Rules and regulations can differ not only from state to state but also from district to district. They need to be carefully checked out and adhered to *before* establishing your business and *before* printing your stationery and business cards. This may sound painfully obvious, yet some brave, or foolish, individuals actually do all that and *then* find their business cannot be conducted from home.

In general, a home-business owner needs to consider the neighbours and the surrounding environment. Will you be making excessive noise with any machinery or polluting the atmosphere? What about parking—are you expecting many clients to be constantly coming and going? This can be annoying for the neighbours. It is essential that you contact the local council and make sure your business will comply with its regulations.

When Anne Procek decided to start a typing service from home, she wrote to the planning department of her local council providing details of her intention. She was to be the only person involved in the business, had a home office with a floor area of 10 square metres and owned a computer, printer, photocopier and fax machine. She intended to collect and deliver work to clients, so there would be no local parking problems. The council confirmed that Anne's business fell into the category of 'home activity' and that no development approval was required. Since Anne was renting her home, she also spoke with her landlord, who gave his assent.

Tom Wilson, who had recently lost his job, set up a car-spraying venture in his backyard. Before long a neighbour complained to the council about the resulting fumes. It warned him to cease operations or vacate the premises in 14 to 21 days—unless he wanted to face legal action which could result in severe penalties, such as a $10,000 fine. Tom decided to call it a day and look for another employer instead of working for himself.

You will also need to find out whether or not you need a business licence. Your state business centre is an ideal source for this information. Its database will contain the names of hundreds of activities that require licences—ranging from beekeeping to emu farming, from interpreting to plumbing, from installing security alarms to making wedding videos.

Robyn Russell knew she would have to have a licence to operate her plumbing business from home, so she consulted her state business centre. She learned that she would need a plumbing worker's registration and a plumbing contractor's licence. Depending on the activities she intended to undertake, she might need other licences: to remove asbestos, perform gas-fitting or install fire sprinkler systems. At the business centre, Robyn picked up all the application forms required, together with details of where they needed to be lodged and at what cost.

Once you have permission to start, you'll need to brush up on your *business skills.* 'I have seen many ventures fail because the owners have no idea of how to run a business,' says Adelaide home-based electrician Bob Flaherty. 'They may know their trade well but the costing, bookkeeping and accounts let them down time after time. One of my rules is for people to do some sort of business course, however basic. I feel very strongly about that.'

'So many people start a business without adequate preparation,' says Professor Alan Williams. 'Three-quarters of them commit the money, commit their ego, and commit their family without talking to anybody! They are undercapitalised—they may be good technically, as a tailor or a builder, but they fail to understand that there is a lot more involved in running a business than carrying out the work of their trade or profession.'

In 20 years of studying small business, Williams has found that the first few months are critical. He says:

> 11 per cent of small businesses fail in the first three months. 18 per cent fail in the first six months. 30 per cent fail by the end of the first year. 39 per cent fail by the end of the second year. 70 per cent fail by the end of the fifth year. And 90 per cent of small businesses fail within 10 years. The remaining 10 per cent are considered high flyers!

Williams says failure is usually the result of a lack of management skills, technical expertise, or entrepreneurial drive. Often, he adds, 'People will say "I ran out of cash". But if you dig deeper, you will find the real causes—lack of sales, poor cost control and so on. When business failure is related to financial management, it can be due to neglecting to realise the significance of liquidity and a good and positive cash flow. You need to do your budgeting, look at what earns the money, keep proper books and records and—beyond this—look at sales and marketing.'

Do *you* have the necessary business skills? If not, you will need, at the very least, to learn bookkeeping for your own records and for taxation purposes. A small business course at your local college or small business centre can provide you with the basics. It can also change your mind about having your own business!

Williams, who runs small business seminars, says a third of those attending subsequently decide against starting up a business.

> Once they get down to the hard facts, they may say 'it's not for me' or they may put it off for a couple of years until they get more experience. Running a business is very, very demanding. It is more than a job, it is a life commitment. You are involved 24 hours a day and the risks are far greater than in a job. There are more emotional demands and more psychological demands. It is like becoming a parent. Anyone can become a parent. To become a *good* parent is more difficult. It is the same with starting up a business—easy to do but more difficult to do well.

As well as skills, you'll need sufficient *capital* with which to start your business. It is also advisable to have personal savings that can tide you over for six months or more as you establish and build up your business. These savings can also be useful further down the track should business suddenly slump—they are your insurance policy, a vital back-up resource. Working for an employer, you did not need to worry about this. Your income was regular and secure. But business fluctuates, up one month and down the next.

In your business plan, estimate a realistic monthly income for yourself. Err on the conservative side and appreciate the fact that at first you may go for some time without any income at all.

'For six, nine or even twelve months after starting your business, most of the money goes *out* the door rather than coming in,' points out Williams. If you decide to make sales on 30 or 60 days' credit you will naturally need to wait that length of time for payment. Do ensure you have strong collection policies in place from the start—you do not want to be waiting indefinitely.

If you go into business with insufficient capital, you are on the fast track to failure. This is where planning is absolutely crucial. Good planning and preparation cannot be stressed enough.

It's just as important to have a team of *professionals you can ask for advice.* You cannot possibly expect to know everything about every aspect of your business. Professionals can tell you about the latest regulations or developments that may affect you. At the very least, build up a good relationship with an accountant, solicitor and bank manager.

If you don't already know such people, you can find them by word-of-mouth recommendation, from a list of names supplied by the professional organisation in question, or from the *Yellow Pages* or a similar directory. Make sure you pick someone who is suitably qualified, with the background and experience you specifically need. They should give value for money, be easy to communicate with, be reliable and consistent, up to date with advice and information and readily contactable.

You are paying for these services, so if you are dissatisfied with your solicitor's arrogant and dismissive attitude or your accountant's constant unavailability, say so, and change professionals! And do check the fee schedule before you commit yourself. You may decide your accountant is not such a friendly, helpful chap after all, once you receive a bill for your chatty telephone conversations—which he deems 'consultations'. Do make sure you know what is and what is not a chargeable service.

Again, your local small business centre can be a helpful source of guidance. But *do* seek professional advice. After all, the experts have experience and knowledge and know of the dangers and pitfalls.

But sometimes it pays to flout the advice and go on gut instinct. Roy Williams, the wetsuit manufacturer, approached a business centre for information on starting up his business. 'They told me that there already was another company in the area and that I would be wasting my time. No one encouraged me at all,' he says.

Roy thought otherwise and, undeterred, approached the bank for a loan, armed with a comprehensive and impressive business plan. 'They had never seen anything like it,' says Roy. 'They bent over backwards to help me.' He was offered a $60,000 overdraft, yet he has never needed more than $10,000. His business has proved extremely successful.

The moral of this story? If you have done the research thoroughly and you believe in yourself and your capabilities, do not allow anyone to put you off.

The business plan

So what is a business plan? Why do you need one? How do you put one together?

Most of us plan our holidays meticulously. We decide where and when we will go and for how long. We have a good idea how much it will cost us, and we browse through brochures and watch videos to find out exactly what we can expect to see and do. We may plan the daytrips we will make, the sightseeing tours, the museums, art galleries and shopping areas we intend to visit.

Do we ever go into this much detail about our *work*? Rarely. Yet, unlike holidays, work takes up the bulk of our days, the majority of our life.

How many of us would think of erecting a house without consulting an architect? Would *you* be content with a general idea, a vague concept, of what you wanted and then expect the builders to learn as they went along?

And if it didn't work out, would you just shrug and return to your old house? Of course not. So how can you possibly expect to start a successful business without a plan?

Just as a house plan covers every component of the structure, so must a business plan cover every aspect of your business. Professor Alan Williams says: 'The reason people do not make a business plan is that most of those starting up businesses are *doers* rather than *thinkers*. They believe making out a business plan is not worth the trouble. They do not see it giving them an immediate return for their efforts. Working day to day, coping with demands and crises on the way, there is no time to plan. And with no planning, problems occur—and they are still there a week, a month or a year later.'

Put aside time to plan, or today's problem will become tomorrow's problem.

'In retrospect, I would have done a small business course and made a business plan,' says computer consultant Wesley

Brown. 'That would have been much easier than learning along the way.'

John Ehm, of Homechain, did make a detailed business plan. He found this paid big dividends.

The business plan is a realistic outline of your company and its projected future. It contains background information, operating information, financial information and marketing information.

You can use your business plan to raise finance for your business, and plan and control your business now and in the future. You should regularly re-evaluate the state of your business and update your business plan accordingly.

Background information

Set out your employment background and that of any partners or employees. What qualifications and experience do you have? What is your business aim, company vision, business philosophy? Compose a mission statement.

Operating information

Give a full description of the nature of the service and product you will offer, together with reasons why clients would select your business over that of your competitors. Outline any manufacturing process, including particulars such as production capacity, cost of raw materials, operating and packaging costs and any other overheads. Describe your premises.

Financial information

How much capital do you require to start your business? Take into account costs of office and other equipment, professional services (accountant, etc.) and so on. Do not underestimate your start-up costs. State where the money will come from—a bank loan, your savings, family money.

Examine your *assets* and *liabilities*. Assets can be broken down into current assets, such as savings, and fixed assets, such as your car and house. Liabilities may be current or fixed, such as food costs and rent or mortgage payments.

Include a *projection of cash flow* for the first year and the following two years. Look at several situations—best case, worst case and an in-between scenario. If, for example, you intend to work from home as a freelance journalist, you will need to consider the number of articles you can realistically produce each week, or fortnight, and balance this against the amount of work available. You need to take into account quiet periods and short breaks or holidays. You need to allow for income fluctuation as editors change, magazines fold and others start up. What remuneration can you reasonably expect? Naturally, these will all be estimates. What costs are involved in earning this income? You will need to include petrol, travel, telephone calls, home-office equipment, postage, stationery and so on. Subtracting costs from income, what are your expected profits? Will this give you an adequate income, one on which you can live comfortably?

Marketing information

Where is your market and how far does it extend—locally, interstate or internationally? How will you reach this market? You need to do thorough research here, examining the past market in your service or product and assessing its future potential.

Your fees and charges will need to be assessed in this part of the business plan. When you work them out, bear in mind the demand for your service or product, manufacturing costs and the prices charged by your competitors. Also, where applicable, estimate the costs of publicity and promotion, which may be done through newspaper, radio and television ads, leaflets or brochures.

Your business plan needs to be professionally presented as well as thoroughly researched. It should be clearly and concisely written, placed in a folder or portfolio and accompanied by drawings, photographs or other illustrations where appropriate. You may prefer to seek professional help in compiling your business plan. Charges vary but you should expect to pay up to several hundred dollars for a fully comprehensive plan. Whatever you decide, though, it's worth the effort—this document, after all, may be worth thousands of dollars in a loan to you!

More detailed information on putting together a business plan can be found in the National Industry Extension Service guide 'Preparing a Business Plan', available from government bookshops and business centres.

How will you operate?

There are several good reasons for choosing to work in your home business in a *part-time* rather than a full-time capacity. The market may not be large enough to be able to provide you with a full income, you may have other commitments which leave you with limited time for your business venture, you may simply not want to work full-time at this enterprise, or you may want to trial the business and ease in gradually to full-time operation. Working at home, you have the option to change your work hours either as you please or as the work dictates.

Whether you gradually ease in to your home business or launch into it at once will depend on your personal circumstances. Some individuals have no choice, having been made redundant or laid off with little or no notice. Others have wanted to start a home business for some time but have been wary. Now they decide to face the fear head-on. There are advantages and disadvantages to both scenarios. Can you afford to take an initial drop in salary? Will you be sitting idle for much of your time, waiting for clients to build up? Why not build up a client base while keeping your present job?

Interior designer Catherine Bugoss realised the company for which she had worked for seven years was collapsing and so she chose to resign. Two months later her employer went into receivership. 'Fortunately I was involved with a network marketing company and so this gave me an income, albeit small,' she says. 'I had always wanted to start my own interior design business but I never had the courage or the funds to do it. The network business gave me confidence, knowledge and finance.' Today Catherine works for herself in interior design, teaming up with a colleague for larger projects.

Others prefer to keep their employment while they slowly build up their customer base and income. That way they avoid a sudden drop in income when they make the switch. I used to be a dentist, and went from full-time to part-time dental work as I gradually built up my writing time from evenings and weekends to three and then four days a week. At the same time I built up my contacts, skills and reputation as a writer. Once I had decided I had enough regular work to provide me with a decent income, I launched into writing full time. But the whole process took several years.

Ross Sutherland also thought long and hard about his career change. When he left his teaching job to join his wife Jan in Dial-A-Wife, the cleaning business had already been established for several years. The couple's detailed business plan told them that Dial-A-Wife would now be able to provide Ross, too, with an appropriate income.

Beate Wickert started her jewellery manufacturing business soon after arriving in Cairns in 1993. 'I used to do this work in Sydney and was initially worried that it would not work here, but figures have doubled in the last year,' she says.

Some people start out in a small way at home, testing the market before launching themselves onto the wider business scene. Some of the world's biggest business success stories started life at home. Apple Computers was born in an Oregon garage in 1976. Kambrook Distributing started from Frank Bannigan's Kambrook Road backyard, Melbourne, in 1964, and is now one of Australia's biggest manufacturers of small electrical appliances.

Starting from home enables you to keep costs down—there are no expensive office rents and associated overheads. If the business does not go as planned, you do not stand to lose so much money.

Running the business

The main ways of running a business are as a sole trader, a partnership, or a limited liability company. Most owners of home businesses are sole traders, but some are partnerships and a few are limited companies.

Operating as a *sole trader* is straightforward. Establishment costs are minimal and establishment time just a few days. You can have others work for you but, as sole proprietor, you and you alone are ultimately responsible for the business. You and the business are one and the same, legally and financially inseparable.

A sole trader has unlimited liability. This means you are personally liable for any debts or claims. Should you burn someone's legs while waxing them in your home beauty salon, you can be sued. Your personal assets—house or car—can be seized and sold in order to settle the claim.

On the other hand, as a sole trader you can greatly reduce your tax bill by deducting legitimate business expenses from your income. You can claim a proportion of the interest on your mortgage and electricity costs for your home office (see Chapter 4). As a sole trader, though, you will have to pay provisional tax. Unlike a limited liability company, a sole trader is not required to hold shareholders' or directors' meetings.

Being in a *partnership* is more complex than being a sole trader but has the advantage that you can involve between two and nineteen other people in the business. The most likely scenario for a home business, however, is two people. In a partnership, you can share the work, the worries and the risk, the start-up capital and the expenses. Yet a partnership can be the easiest way of turning a friend into an enemy! Even when working with a spouse, it is highly advisable to seek legal advice and then draw up a formal partnership agreement.

Like a sole trader, a partnership is relatively easy to set up, run and wind up. There are also similarities in the legal and tax positions. But if you are considering this option, bear in mind that while each partner is personally liable, any debt or claim goes to the partnership. So, should your partner burn a client's legs while waxing them, *you* can be held responsible. If your partner runs off or has no money, *your* assets are on the line.

There are other practical matters to think of when contemplating a partnership. How well do you get on with the other person? Do you trust the other person and have confidence in their skills and abilities? How will the work and profits be divided? Are both of your signatures required on any cheques? What happens if one partner decides to leave?

As with a marriage, enter into such an agreement in haste and repent at your leisure!

To set up a *limited liability company* requires an understanding of corporations law, so you will need the assistance of a solicitor and an accountant. A limited liability company is complicated to set up, run and wind up. Establishment costs are greater and establishment time is longer.

The main advantage of a limited liability company is that as a legal entity it is separate from its owners. Liability is limited to its assets. If an employee of Bella's Beauty Secrets burns someone's legs with hot wax, the company is liable but the total loss is limited to the company's assets. Bella's personal property is safe.

A limited liability company requires at least two officers—one director, who is also a shareholder, and a company secretary. There can be up to 50 owners. Certain rules must also be adhered to, such as holding regular directors' and shareholders' meetings and keeping records of these meetings.

Naming the business

Registration of a business name is not a legal requirement if you are working under your own name but is compulsory once you start trading under another name. It can be worthwhile in either case, as a business name can get you noticed and add to your professional image.

You can use any name provided it is not already registered by someone else. Jane Eastern Publishing or Brunswick Plumbing Services immediately identifies you, your business and your locality. When photographer Matt Turner started his home business, he operated under the name of Your Choice Photography. Talking to colleagues, he realised that using his own name instead would boost both his profile and his reputation as a photographer. This has worked for him. People notice his name under his pictures in newspapers and magazines, associate that name with good work and hire Matt Turner, Photographer for their next project.

Procedures and fees for registering a business name vary from state to state. The application form needs to be completed by *all* individuals associated with your business.

Certain words are not allowed to be used as part of a business name in Australia. There is a long list, including 'corporative', 'consumer', 'America's Cup', and 'club'. When Anna Pyrzakowski applied to register the name Design Club for her interior design business, she was told this term is approved for use only by sporting bodies and associations.

A business name can add an air of mystery and intrigue to your occupation. When John from *Our Father's Electrical Service* came to attend to the flickering picture on my television screen, I asked how long the home-based business had been in the family. He looked perplexed. 'Didn't your father start it?' I asked. He smiled. For it turned out that the 'father' in question was 'Our Lord'—rather than a blood relation! John could not find anything wrong with my television set and did not even charge me. I was impressed. Especially as ever since John laid his hands on it, my TV has behaved perfectly!

Trade marks and patents

Have you looked closely at a bottle of Coca-Cola? The *trade mark* is the familiar swirling script, and the liquid contents are protected by a *patent* and the *design* is the unique old-fashioned glass bottle.

If you want to apply for a trade mark or patent, you can get forms and details from your local branch of the Australian Industrial Property Organisation. For advice on how and whether to proceed, you will need to consult professionals such as patent and intellectual property lawyers.

Standards

Your business may need to comply with one or more of the 6000-plus standards imposed by law on Australian products. Timber framing standards, for example, are set down in the Building Code of Australia. Your industry or trade governing body or the Standards Australia Information Centre in Sydney or Melbourne can help you with further details.

Franchises

A franchise is the granting of a licence by the franchisor to a franchisee that entitles the franchisee to the use of the trade mark, trade name and business package to reproduce the system. Some franchises, such as the lawnmowing services Jim's Mowing or VIP Mowing, can be run from home.

Buying into a franchise can be a quick and relatively secure way of starting up a small business, especially for someone with limited business experience. The success rate of franchises—note, though, that these are by no means all home-based—is twice that of other small businesses. Joining a good franchise provides you with a ready pool of clients, managerial skills, a bookkeeping system and ongoing help and advice. You are, of course, joining an established and, presumably, successful business. The initial expense is offset by the lower risk entailed in joining an established business. Obviously it is still up to you and your capabilities, but you are starting with a better chance of future success. A franchise can also be a good start for those intending to go into business for themselves later. One of the drawbacks of joining a franchise is that you need to be prepared to stick to a system that is already in place. This may not suit some individuals.

Once you apply to buy into a franchise and have approval, the franchisor will sell you the right to the service or product, the use of the business name and logo, and the right to trade for a set number of years—usually five or ten. After your initial outlay, you may be required to pay regular fees or to buy product or equipment only from the franchisor so as to ensure consistent quality and service. In return, you are entitled to advice and back-up service from franchise headquarters.

In selecting a franchise, ask yourself:

- How long has the franchisor been operating and what is the company's reputation?
- Is the franchisor registered with the Franchisors Association of Australia and New Zealand Limited, and does it adhere to the Franchising Code of Practice? Such registration is not compulsory but is certainly advisable.
- Have you spoken with other franchisees in this company?
- Are you interested enough in this service or product to want to work in the field?
- What is the public image of this service or product?
- Will the work be seasonal and, if so, can you survive on the income or supplement it in other ways?
- Is the right to an area or territory exclusive to you?
- Is there potential for growth?
- How much will the franchise cost—now and later?
- What does this price include?
- Are there good back-up services and advice?

- Will you have to buy your product or equipment from the franchisor?

If you are considering buying into a franchise, it is worthwhile making contact with the Franchise Association of Australia and New Zealand Limited. A good starting point is reading its publication 'The Franchisee's Guide'. The Franchise Association of Australia and New Zealand Limited can be contacted on (612) 9891 4933. If you do go ahead, make sure you study the franchise contract in detail.

A GROWING CONCERN

'My philosophy is, "If you love what you're doing, you'll never work a day in your life," ' says Phil Maunder.

And if you love mowing lawns and gardening, you're made! As South Australian manager for Jim's Mowing, Phil is convinced that franchises are an ideal introduction to small business.

'Many of our people come from middle management,' he explains. 'They may be skilled in one area, such as management or marketing, but they have not worked for themselves before. What a lot of people find difficult is that when you run your own business, you need to be good at everything—doing the bookwork and preparing the invoices, finding clients and marketing, collecting accounts and so on—*as well as doing your job.*

'That means franchises are a good start for a lot of people. We do the work in setting up, training, advertising and back-up and, in one week rather than a few months, you can be working in an established business. The process and the speed of getting a business up and running are done for you. You are buying a name—Jim's Mowing—that is well known to the general public. Moreover, when you are sick or on holiday, trained people are available to take over your work.'

What sort of people take up this lawnmowing franchise? 'Until eighteen months ago, more than half of our franchisees had been retrenched or had taken early retirement. They found the money was insufficient and they needed to have an income. That has all changed now, we see fewer people with redundancy packages. These days, people approach Jim's Mowing because they want to work for themselves. They are not forced to find work, and this makes them better operators.'

Phil believes the key to success is enjoying what you are doing and having an affinity for it. 'You can like mowing lawns, but when you do so day in and day out, to put bread and butter on your table, it becomes a different proposition.'

Franchisees need a good personality. 'People who get on with the clients generally do very well. You can do a wonderful job, but unless you get on with the clients, they will not notice it. What's more, if the clients don't like you and you do one tiny thing unsatisfactorily in their eyes, they will cancel.'

Phil started off as a franchisee himself, in Melbourne. When others told him he would find it a lonely job, he was not unduly worried. 'But I found it was. There were no co-workers to talk to during the day and there was no feedback.' He found such support, and a level of commitment, back at the main office. 'The role of the franchisor is to talk to the franchisee,' he says, 'to be a sounding-board. To be successful, you need to have a good relationship, not just a business relationship, but also an ability to get on well together.'

The first step in acquiring a Jim's Mowing franchise is to have an interview. If both parties are satisfied, the potential franchisee is then sent out on a 'field day' with an experienced trainer who supplies a written report on the personality, attitude and motivation of the individual. 'The main thing we look at, in addition to the personality, is the improvement in the standard and quality of the work throughout that day.'

Once approved, the individual can purchase a Jim's Mowing franchise for ten years, renewable for a further ten years. 'This is a good way to find your feet in business,' says Phil. 'After some years, a proportion of our franchisees sell out and go on to set up their own businesses.'

Russell Botten bought a Jim's Mowing franchise. He'd never worked for himself; his previous experience was in clerical duties and hotel management. 'I had a passion for gardening and then I saw a television ad for franchises which described this as "buying yourself a job". It seemed like a reasonable way of earning a living to me. I was not confident enough to go out as a private contractor and I did not have the resources to build up a client base,' explains Russell, 'so I decided to look at going under the umbrella of a franchise.'

'Buying himself a job' cost Russell just over $20,000 in 1995, plus $4,000 for equipment—a lawnmower, tools and a trailer. The price for the franchise area was negotiable and was based on the number of clients. 'Someone was selling off his area and Jim's Mowing held on to his money for four weeks before paying him until I was satisfied I was getting all the customers I had paid for.'

Russell bought—and wears—the standard Jim's Mowing uniform, was supplied with a training manual and attends regular training seminars. These cover various aspects of work—lawn care and pruning—and there are additional practical sessions. At these times, Russell has an opportunity to meet with other franchisees and share his experiences. This all began after his initial training and the time he spent on his round learning from the previous franchisee.

While Russell took out a loan to buy in to Jim's Mowing, there are other possibilities—working for Jim's Mowing for a set income or as a subcontractor for someone like Russell. Russell is pleased with his decision to join Jim's Mowing. He has seen his business grow steadily from month to month—in fact he has tripled his client base in just one year—and he has plans to buy into other territories.

Most of the year, he works from 8 a.m. until 5 p.m. five-and-a-half to six days a week. 'The work is not really seasonal,' he says, 'it just changes. In the winter, I'll be cleaning out gutters and pruning trees and doing less lawnmowing.'

He enjoys working essentially for himself, not having to answer to anyone, and making his own hours. 'I set myself goals, such as to increase my customer base by a certain amount by next spring, and I stick to this. So far, I have achieved all of my goals. I pay Jim's Mowing a certain amount and they in turn supply me with an area exclusive to me, the training, the bookkeeping methods and the advertising. I can go to them if I have problems, the office is there to give me guidance and advice. And I also have the option of making more money, by selling off part of my area once I have built it up.

'It was a little intimidating, and a little difficult, for me to get a loan. I needed to have the right security, I put my house up as collateral. I do not think I would have got the money had I been renting. You see, I had no experience in business. Now I feel I am much better informed and more confident. A franchise is like a halfway stop. It is an important start for someone who has never worked for himself before.'

Jim's Mowing is Australia's largest lawnmowing franchise, with over 1,000 franchisees at last count. Started in 1989 by Jim Penman in Victoria, it is one of the fastest-growing businesses in Australia.

Jim admits he is not perfect. 'There are things I am not good at, such as people skills. I get impatient and irritable, and accounting is also my bugbear. But I am a pretty good delegator,' he says. 'Anyone who works for me has to be better at that job than I am. I always employ people better than myself!'

For those interested in franchises, and the history of Jim's Mowing, *The Cutting Edge* by Jim Penman, printed in Australia by The Book Printer, 1992 and available from any office of Jim's Mowing, offers a detailed, insightful and down-to-earth read.

FROM A DREAM TO REALITY

When Peter Robertson was left a paraplegic at 21 after a motorcycle accident in 1980, he thought his work prospects were drastically reduced. Working as a production control clerk for an Adelaide stationery manufacturer, he had become more and more dissatisfied, wanting to make use of his artistic abilities. 'I had originally wanted to be an architect,' he says. After his accident, Peter spent six months in hospital and six months in rehabilitation. 'I was then able to return to my job. They made certain modifications for me, ramps to allow for wheelchair access and handrails in the toilet. It was good going back to the same place. But you also face the fact that you are not able to do the same things, reach for things, have the same access. I felt conspicuous for a while, having to duck and weave in a wheelchair instead of being almost 2 m tall.'

He persevered for a few years and then decided to follow his dream. After spending a year studying for adult matriculation, he approached HETA—Handicapped Employment Training Assistance—and was shown how to go about finding work. 'I sent out masses of letters applying for work experience in drafting to facilitate future employment. One company replied, "If you can get here despite your disability, we will accept you". I can walk a bit so I would pull myself up the stairs in that building while someone carried my wheelchair,' recalls Peter. He spent three months tracing and copying from drawings and then started being offered small paid packages of work: drawing up the mechanical details of rollers for an extender conveyor belt, teeth for mining equipment, pipelines. He was subsequently subcontracted to work at the Housing Trust of South Australia and concurrently undertook a four-year drafting course.

'I left the company, as I found myself in an inequitable financial situation,' Peter explains. A significant proportion of his wages was being paid to the company that had subcontracted him. Peter approached the Housing Trust for work independently and continued working there on contract for some years. 'Then their money ran out so I started working from home. It was difficult. My first year, earnings were negligible. It was a toss-up between the dole and work. The weeks I had paid work, I told Social Security and it resulted in very messy paperwork and not a lot of money.' Then a friend told Peter of NEIS, the New Enterprise Incentive Scheme. Having fulfilled the entry criteria, he attended the six-week course and was then 'subsidised to the tune of unemployment benefits on a fortnightly basis for a year', by which time his business was established.

'It was much better being on unemployment benefit,' says Peter, 'as whatever you earn does not affect this payment. Your partner's income is taken into consideration. You get regular payments rather than a lump sum, which can be a problem, but luckily my business did not require a large cash outlay.' Another bonus of the scheme was to provide Peter with a business mentor, with whom he remains in contact.

The final task in the six-week course was to prepare and present a business plan on which the decision about future financing depended. Peter decided to give his design/drafting business a focus on the aged and disabled. 'You need to show you are not just the same as a million other drafting businesses,' he reasons, 'and I can design with an empathy for such clients.'

To look in more detail at his business, Peter used a S.W.O.T. analysis in his business plan. This tackled Strengths, Weaknesses, Opportunities and Threats. Peter saw his business as giving him a fulfilling and financially secure career at home and, among his strengths, he included the pride he took in his work, his concern with customer satisfaction and the fact that his work could be produced at highly competitive rates due to low office overheads.

Working from a compact home office, he deals in both commercial and residential projects. He's worked on suburban Adelaide units, a city hotel, and a basketball stadium at Oodnadatta. 'I can work at home easily,' he says. 'Outside offices may have to make modifications for me.' Another advantage to Peter of being home-based is spending time with his wife, Marilyn, and nine-year-old daughter, Leah. Marilyn works as a theatre sister and, Peter says, feels she has lost some of her autonomy with him being constantly at home. 'So I will spend one day a week outside. On Fridays I will make site visits, drop off printing, get plans and titles from town. It is more efficient for me to do all this in one day and it gives freedom to Marilyn.'

3

HOME SWEET OFFICE

When Mil Clay started working as a desktop publisher from his Cairns home, he used the open-plan main living area as his office. His large wooden desk, computer and printer are at one end of the room, while the fax machine and telephone are a few metres away, at the kitchen end. Having no separate work space 'does not bother me', says Mil, 'but it concerns my wife, Annette.' Mil says Annette finds it irritating to be cooking alongside her husband while he works. She is also unhappy about work calls outside normal business hours and the fact that Mil's hours often intrude into family time with their two children. So Mil now plans to move his workstation to the back of the house.

Obviously most people would prefer to avoid problems like Mil's. But some have no alternative but to work in their home's living area, at least at first. One advantage of the situation, in Mil's view, is that it has forced him to be compact and organised. His sturdy wooden desk is about 150 cm long, with drawer space on both sides. Three stackable plastic trays provide additional filing space on his desk. A calendar is clipped to the front of them. Mil sits in front of a Mac LC 630 computer, above which a couple of wooden wall shelves hold reference books and other resources. His laser printer sits on a two-drawer metal filing cabinet to his left. He has a comfortable and adjustable office chair on castors and is kept cool by both an overhead and a small portable fan. The most enviable part of Mil's home office is the glorious view to his right. Glass sliding doors open onto a wide wooden balcony overlooking green palms and distant hills. Who would opt for the sterile environment of an airconditioned office if this was the alternative?

Wayne Ketchen's home office is a dream. As an architect, he was able to design it specifically for his needs. The space is large enough to accommodate his four desks and drawing boards, fax machine, photocopier and computer. Natural light is most important for his work, so Wayne has installed large windows along one side of the room. On the opposite wall, shelves are filled with his manuals and books. His home office is located away from the living area of the house. Recently, Wayne sold his drawing boards and installed CAD (computer-aided design) in his work practice, thus giving himself more space in his office.

Desktop publisher Maggie Boday has put aside a room in her Melbourne house for a home office, yet it is far from ideal. 'On entering, you fall over my scanner,' she laughs, 'and then you bump into my desk. You can't open the door properly because my husband Frank has bought a new filing cabinet and there is a big photocopier pushed under one desk.' The office is also home to a couple of computers and three printers. Space is not just tight, it is desperately inadequate. Does this sound familiar?

Jeffrey Frith is an architect and ergonomist. Past president of the Ergonomics Society of Australia, he is regarded as an expert in workplace design and currently works as a private consultant in this field. He is a former chairman of the committee which developed Australian Standards 3590 part 2, looking at appropriate workstation furniture for people performing screen-based tasks. 'You will save yourself a lot of heartache and anguish if you consult someone before setting up your home office,' he advises.

Frith says there are three aspects to consider in setting up a home office: the work environment, the work tools and equipment and the work system.

The work environment

When you work from home, there tends to be a blur between work and home life. 'If you are a workaholic, it can be difficult for you to switch off. This situation can be like an alcoholic with a gin bottle—you can't stop,' says Frith. This blur can be overcome by having a designated area or room for your work and by reducing distracting influences—pets, children, partner—during your working hours.

If at all possible, a separate home office is best both for yourself and for those you live with because it:

- makes your work life more organised, efficient and hence more productive;
- allows you to have clear and well-defined working hours;
- gives you a psychological boost—you *work* here, the office is not the place for social chats or cups of coffee; and
- creates a discrete physical space, which permits you to close the door, leaving the outside world—or your work—behind.

Having set aside your work space, you should give careful thought to its lighting, design and set-up. It may be worth paying a professional to advise you here. You will be spending much of your time in your home office, so make the most of it. A cold, bare room will hardly encourage you to work. A few well-placed posters, pot plants, rugs and paintings can make the space more appealing.

Clever use of colour can help create a more pleasant and comfortable work environment. Building designer Elvio Ferrara chose light yellow for his table-tops, as he finds this shade puts less strain on his eyes. The terracotta floor tiles with the blue and black Norwood border please him in another way. 'They are the same colours as my favourite football team—Inter Milan,' he says, 'and every time I look at them, I feel good.'

Melbourne physiotherapist and ergonomist Jacquie Wissenden believes the colour of a room does not affect

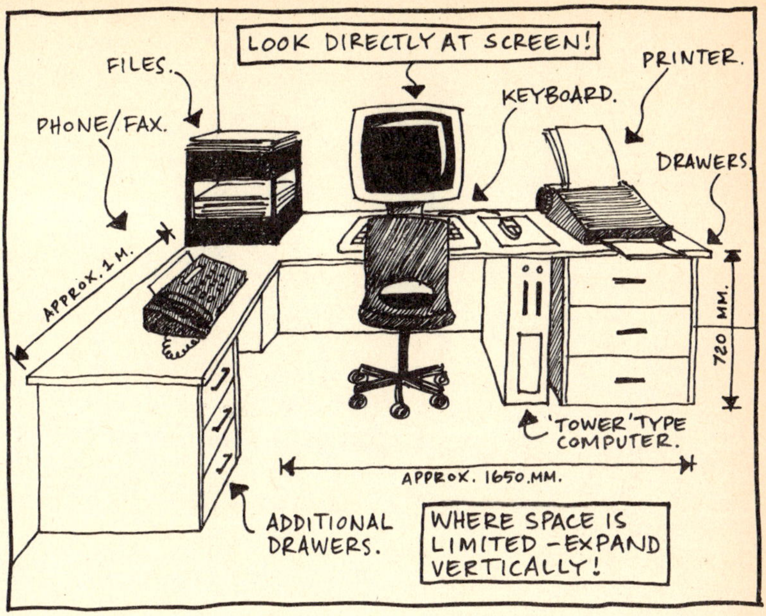

people greatly. 'You will find it mentioned in interior design and ergonomics books that red is a stimulating colour while blue is boring, but I don't believe it makes much difference. Besides, you get used to bright colours. You will hardly notice your striking red hallway after a year. On balance', she adds, 'I would go for neutral tones.'

Climate control is another important consideration. When selecting heaters, bear in mind that fan heaters can be noisy; you may prefer a quieter model. If you choose a bar radiator, don't put it where it can come into contact with liquids such as water or spilt coffee. Curtains and blinds can help insulate the room and minimise glare.

Lighting is very important. Poor lighting can lead to eyestrain and headaches. Make sure overhead or natural light doesn't reflect in your computer screen. Anti-glare screens interfere with text clarity and should be used only as a last resort.

As for your office, some people seem to thrive in a cluttered environment. Albert Einstein agreed his university

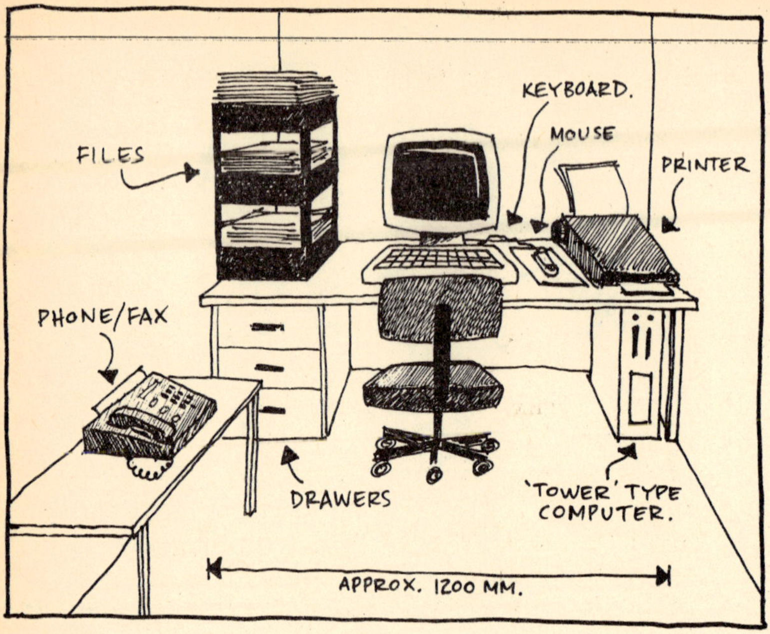

office was chaos but described it as 'organised chaos'. For the rest of us, creativity may be enhanced by a sense of order in the office.

Working tools and equipment

The precise set-up and equipment you need will depend on what type of business you are in, and how big your business is. Some of the items listed below may not be appropriate for you. Not every home-based business needs a personal computer, for example. *Let common sense coupled with your budget and your needs be your guide.* Bear in mind that you can expand or reduce, exchange or upgrade your office equipment as time goes on.

Second-hand equipment will save money, but 'buyer beware', especially with computer and electronic equipment. Buy from a reputable source. Getting things at garage sales can be false economy.

Office equipment: a checklist

- Door that closes (and locks)—this may be the single most important item!
- Desk
- Desk return
- Desk lamp
- Chair—for yourself. Do not economise here
- Chairs for clients
- Accessories
- Telephone. Do you require separate business and private lines? A mobile telephone?
- Answering machine/service and/or pager
- Fax machine
- Photocopier—optional
- Typewriter
- Personal computer and printer
- Filing cabinets
- Extras: noticeboard or whiteboard, shelves and cupboards, wastepaper basket

Door

Closing the door can both save your sanity and boost your work output. If your work space has no door, create some other physical separator—a screen or a curtain. Enter your home office at the start of your day and close the door behind you to prevent interruptions. Productivity rises! Exit your home office at the end of the day and close the door behind you to forget work. Sanity returns with a balanced life—work and play!

It does take some discipline to keep the door closed after work, though—avoiding the temptation to check whether any faxes have come through or responding to early-morning brainwaves. Still, you can build some flexibility into your work hours. That, after all, is why you have chosen to work from home. The main thing is to ensure that your work does not detrimentally impinge on your relationship, family life or time for relaxation. Keith Bainbridge, who runs a home-based credit control service, says, 'If I am worried about work deadlines

I can close the door to separate myself from family. And if things get really desperate, I can lock it!'

Desk

When buying your desk and other office furniture, first look at your available space. Measure it and have the dimensions with you when you go shopping. Don't forget to measure the width of the doorway and entrance hall as well. If you find a desk that seems slightly too big for the doorway, perhaps it can be disassembled or the drawers can be removed. An office furniture supplier I know puts a desk upright on a rug, which can then be spun round to manoeuvre the desk into the room.

You may prefer a desk with a completely level surface or one with an adjustable 'shelf' for a keyboard. This section can be situated on the left, on the right or in the middle of the desk. The choice is yours but must be made when you buy the desk. Adjusting the height of your work surface makes good ergonomic sense. Do it while you adjust the height of your chair. When sitting well in and upright, your hips should be square to your knees and your shoulders square to your hips. Slumping forwards will lead to pain in your shoulders. If you are less than 150 cm tall, you will need to lower the keyboard so your hands are at the correct typing level—elbow height (for writing, the desk surface should be just *above* elbow height). You may also need a foot rest. If you are much taller than average, you may need to raise your whole desk on wood blocks to give you a comfortable work position. The standard desk height is 720 mm, but you can have one custom made if necessary.

You will also need to decide on the configuration of drawers: should you have three drawers, or just one drawer? I have found that paper multiplies to fill every available space. Start off with one filing cabinet and it is soon filled. Start off with three and they are also crammed full very promptly! You just can't win.

A basic office desk of melamine-covered particleboard, with drawers, costs about $300. A top-of-the-range walnut desk can cost $1,500. When making your choice, you should consider whether your office will be seen by clients. Conventional desks are designed for typewriters. A computer screen, however, is ideally placed at arm's distance. Sit too close and you will end up with eyestrain. So look for a deep desk. You should place the terminal so the top is level with your eyebrows, so your natural gaze falls to the middle of the screen. If the screen is set too high, you will tend to open your eyes more widely, which will dry them out. Conversely, if the screen is too low, you will find yourself bending your neck forwards, which will result in neck and shoulder pain.

Desk return

The desk return, an extension attached to one side of the desk, affords extra surface space to hold your printer or for spreading out work, as well as storage space in the way of drawers. Some people also incorporate a typist's pedestal in the return: slots in which you can store papers. Desk returns come in different widths and may be right- or left-handed. Personal preference and room layout will influence your choice.

Desk lamp

This is an optional extra and depends on your requirements. Some professionals, such as architects and draftspeople, *must* have one; others may prefer to add to or improve their overhead or natural lighting.

Chair

After a door, a height-adjustable chair is your most important office item. After all, you will be sitting in it for many hours each day. There are two main types of office chair—the conventional gas- or manual-lift chair, and the Balans chair.

The *Balans chair* is the strange-looking kind into which you kneel. Many people swear by it; many others swear *at* it. A sedentary lifestyle tends to shorten the hamstrings and quadriceps (thigh muscles). So for some, kneeling into a Balans chair, which stretches the quadriceps, can be uncomfortable. But interior designer Catherine Bugoss says she would be lost without her Balans chair. 'I feel completely relaxed and at ease in it,' she says, 'and it forces me to keep my back straight as I draw, which prevents aches and pains.'

If you are considering buying such a chair, ask whether you can hire it overnight and try it out. Many office-furniture stores will be happy to oblige. Alternatively, spend plenty of time in the shop. 'One woman spent three hours deciding between two chairs before she finally made her decision,' says Terry Black of Colin Murch Office Equipment in Adelaide, 'and she was very happy with the one she bought.' There's no point spending anything from $270 to $700 on a chair if it hurts your back more than the old kitchen chair! For the same reason, do not allow anyone else to buy a chair on your behalf. 'A mother came in alone wanting to buy a chair for her daughter,' says Terry. 'That was pointless as her daughter needed to try out any chair herself, for comfort and suitability.'

As the name suggests, *gas lift chairs* can be raised and lowered by a mixture of gas and oil in a cylinder, which forces the seat up or, when compressed by your weight, allows it to drop. The gas-lift chair has two levers—one adjusting the back of the chair and the other tilting the seat. It is vital that this type of chair have a five-way base, that is, *five* wheels. A chair with four wheels will topple over when you lean backwards—not recommended! (These are now banned, but you may come across them at auctions or garage sales.) With a five-way base, whichever way you turn or lean, there is one wheel behind you.

In *manual-lift chairs* the seat can be raised, lowered, and moved backwards or forwards by manually adjusting screws and levers. Although these are about $100 cheaper than gas-lift chairs, demand for them has decreased.

If you get one, you should have no problem if it is to be used by one person at all times. But if another person of a different height will also be using the chair, you will continually need to change the height of the seat. This takes time and can be inconvenient.

When you sit in your chair, your arms should be at thigh level, bent at right angles to your body. But most people prop their arms on the *arm rests.* These are usually at a fixed height. Some chairs now have height-adjustable arm rests but these are dearer. Do you need arm rests? Terry Black says their main use is to help you get in and out of the chair. Unless you have a job that requires the use of arm rests—for arm support while taking notes, for example—forget them. You can rest your arms on the desk, not on the chair, and arm rests prevent you from getting in close to the desk.

Resist the temptation to buy a big '*power*' chair. 'People say to themselves, "I'm running my own business, I'm the boss" and demand an armchair-like "manager" or "executive" chair,' says Terry. 'This may look impressive, but it has poor back support so you are forced to lean forwards. Select a chair with separate back and base so that each can be adjusted,' he advises. 'Do not buy a single, integrated unit.' Bear in mind that for an additional $10 to $20 you can usually get a large rather than a medium-sized back on your chair. You may desire this extra back support.

Where finances permit, *buy a new chair*. This will come with a warranty for two to five years. Buying a second-hand chair is risky. You are not to know whether a 115 kg or a 50 kg person has been sitting in it. How can you tell whether it has been stressed to its upper limits for all of its life? In any case, you will not be saving that much. Even if you pay 30 per cent less, you have no warranty and may well end up with a dud chair.

Chairs for clients

You may or may not need additional chairs for clients. If you do, remember they will only be visiting you briefly, so there is no need for their chairs to be of the same quality as yours. Comfortable, attractive chairs will suffice.

Accessories

Depending on your height and the height of your desk, you may need a *foot rest.* When buying one, make sure you can change the angle. Prices range from $25 to $40. However, ideally your feet should be flat on the floor. This also means you can move your seat around. So wherever possible, adjust desk and chair height rather than rely on a foot rest.

You may want a *chair mat* to protect the floor and to let you roll your chair about more easily. It can also prevent static build-up but this is a minor consideration unless you are constantly using your computer and have a nylon carpet. (If you stand on a nylon carpet and pick up a computer diskette, a discharge of static electricity can wipe it clean.) Chair mats come in three different sizes and range in price from $50 to $200. You can have a small mat for your chair alone, a medium-sized one that extends under the desk, or a larger one that fits under both desk and return. Top-of-the-range mats are made of clear heavy plastic and are anti-static. Cheaper mats are not anti-static, but if you have a timber or tiled floor this feature is unnecessary. Here the mat is solely to protect the floor from being scratched by your chair. If you have carpet, check its thickness. Piles of 16 mm and deeper require a thicker and heavier chair mat. Buy a cheaper thinner type and the chair mat will crack due to lack of support. The ideal support for a chair mat is a concrete floor covered by a thin underlay and then a carpet.

An *anti-glare* screen will reduce the reflection of overhead lighting in your computer screen. An optical glass screen, at about $90, is anti-static and can also cut down radiation glare. At the other end of the scale, you can buy what is essentially a glorified flywire screen for $9. The best idea is to position your lighting, or computer, so you do not get glare off the screen in the first place.

A *copy holder* improves posture and is advisable when reading at your desk and typing. It can be placed on either side of your computer screen or between the computer screen and keyboard, and angled so that your head is in a neutral position while you read and type. If you lay documents flat on your desk, you will need to bend and twist to read them.

There are about a dozen varieties. One model, from $18, is supported at its back, holds your material upright and can be pushed to one side. Another model, from $40 to $80, consists of a hinged adjustable arm arrangement and is mounted on the edge of your desk with a clamp. It can therefore be placed directly over your keyboard, which is ideal from an ergonomic point of view.

Browsing around office equipment shops will introduce you to a number of other accessories—adjustable monitor stands which enable you to position your computer screen in the optimum spot, adjustable wrist supports to reduce stress and fatigue. Once you have the essentials, you can put such extras on your birthday or Christmas wish lists!

Telephone

Something as straightforward as selecting a telephone and the accompanying services is becoming increasingly complex. Not only are there many types of phone, but today there is the added complication of choosing a service provider—Telstra, Optus or one of the many telephone resellers. Offers and prices are constantly changing, so it is worth a little investigation before making your choice.

Whichever service provider you select, Telstra will charge you a quarterly 'service and equipment' fee. Bear this in mind when comparing prices. Your phone bill may well look cheaper with another company, but remember, it does not include your telephone rental. Check who is responsible for any repairs or faults. Will this be Telstra or the other company? Telstra sends out quarterly accounts. Other companies may bill you monthly. Is this a problem for you?

While deregulation has given you more confusion and frustration along with the wider choice, it may ultimately give you a better financial deal. You, as the client, can be the winner from increased competition. And don't be afraid to change companies when circumstances warrant it.

If you can afford it, and your situation would make it useful, install a *separate business line*. This will make your entire operation more professional in an instant. When *this* telephone rings, you will immediately know it is for business and be able to confidently say, 'Brunswick Plumbing Services' without having a friend laugh. The other telephone, your private line, will be freed up for your partner and children—no more arguments there. In addition, you can easily monitor your business telephone expenses, as you will receive a separate bill.

If you have only one line, you must separate the charges for private and business calls. Note your STD calls and check them against your itemised telephone account. Your accountant will ask you to estimate what percentage of your calls are for business purposes. This should not be too difficult. If your phone bill is regularly in the order of $100 and increases to $200 once you start working from home, then you know that 50 per cent of your calls are for business.

A new option, recently introduced by Telstra, is a single line with different ringing tones for social and business calls.

This can save you the expense of a separate line, but you'll need to give out different phone numbers to friends and clients.

Wherever possible, have a dedicated fax line—that is, a separate line for your fax machine. That way, you will be able to talk on the phone while keeping your fax line free and send faxes while keeping your phone line free.

Special phone features are ever-increasing. One useful service for your business may be 'call waiting'. When you are talking on the telephone, a series of beeps indicates that someone else is calling. By putting the first caller on hold, you can speak to the second caller. The advantage of 'call waiting' is that you do not miss out on any calls. Previously, if your line was engaged, the person might not have called back and you might have missed out on business. This function can be switched on and off very easily if you find it a distraction after hours or at weekends.

'Call waiting' does have its drawbacks. It can be frustrating and inconvenient to interrupt one telephone conversation and go to another. It can also be expensive—if the second caller is from interstate and you arrange to call back, whose telephone bill goes up? My experience is that 'call waiting' acts as a magnet, attracting other callers. The telephone will be silent for a couple of hours and then, just when I go to make a call, three people will call me, one after the other. My all-time classic was switching to accept the second call just as my fax machine swung into action *and* the front doorbell rang! I could leave the fax machine to its own devices, but if I'd had a mobile telephone I could have walked to the door and dealt with the delivery while still attending to my caller!

A *mobile telephone* can be vital for your business. It lets clients contact you anywhere and at any time. As Adelaide electrician Bob Flaherty puts it, 'If people have a need for your product or service, you need to be able to respond'. There are two types of mobile, or cellular, phone: analogue and digital. You can compare them to the Beta and VHS video cassette systems. Both work but one is soon to be outdated. Analogue telephones will cease operation completely on 1 January 2000. Do such phones have any advantages? Yes. Their reach is presently marginally better. However, unless you are spending a lot of time in outlying country areas this should not make much difference to you. They are cheaper, and you can have one connected for $10 a month. Mind you, you can then pay up to $1.50 a minute for calls compared with 38 cents for calls on a digital phone with a network access fee of $35 a month. Remember: *The cheaper the access plan, the higher the call rate.*

A mobile telephone can cost from $69, for the cheapest analogue, to $1,300 for the most expensive digital model, which can be used overseas and connected to your computer. On top of that cost, you pay the monthly network access charge and also your call charges. Some businesspeople use their mobile telephone only for incoming calls. That way, they keep costs to a minimum.

Depending on which dealer you go to, you will be automatically connected to their related service: Optus, Telstra or Vodafone (digital only), etc. You may choose your dealer on this basis, as fees and charges—and coverage—differ.

Answering machine

My answering machine paid for itself with the very first call it recorded. It was an editor, ringing to commission a magazine article. I was able to get back to her promptly and accept the offer. The fee covered the cost of the machine.

As with other items of office equipment, there are many answering machines on the market. Which one will suit you—a no-frills model for less than $100 or a more sophisticated one with a voice-activated remote control that costs several hundred dollars? Do not be swayed by fancy extras. Ask yourself first if you really need them. If you are frequently out for much of the day and would find it useful to be able to pick up your messages remotely, by all means look at answering machines that offer this option. Otherwise, look for a machine that makes good quality voice recordings—your outgoing message is part of your professional image—and is reliable. There will certainly be models within your price range, but beware: as the saying goes, 'The bitterness of poor quality remains long after the sweetness of the cheap price has faded.' In other words, you get what you pay for!

Fax machine

According to the Roy Morgan Research Centre, as of June 1996 8 per cent of Australians had a fax machine at home. Three years before it was 5 per cent. The fax machine enables documents of all kinds, including diagrams and pictures, to be transmitted instantaneously from one point to another, whether that be across the street, across the country or across time zones. It has revolutionised both the way in which we communicate and the speed with which we do so. With a fax modem connected to your personal computer, you can bypass the fax machine and transfer information from one computer to another, eliminating the use of paper altogether.

Check out the range of fax machines available, selecting according to your budget and needs. A basic model where each page has to be fed in singly by hand can be bought second-hand for $300. This may be all you require. At the other end of the scale, you can pay $2,000 for a machine that uses plain (not heat-sensitive) paper, sends several pages automatically, cuts pages as they come in, and redials if a number is engaged. Perhaps you don't need to buy a fax machine at all. Can you share a machine with a nearby colleague or pay to send and receive faxes at the local post office or business-services shop?

Computer

Pat Golotta wanted to buy a computer but found herself becoming more and more confused with each store she visited. The salespeople bamboozled her with incomprehensible information and she started to doubt her ability to use the machine at all—even if she ever did make a decision about buying one. For those who have never used a computer, the prospect can be a daunting experience. Compare it to driving a car. If you have never driven, it can seem difficult. But once you have mastered the essentials and had some practice, it comes automatically.

The first question to ask yourself is whether you need a computer. Perhaps you don't need one yet. Perhaps you will never need one. What would a computer do for you that you cannot presently do? Or what would a computer do for you more simply, more efficiently and more quickly?

As a freelance journalist, I cannot imagine life without a computer. These days, I can quickly and easily edit my articles, change paragraph and sentence order swiftly, and rapidly print out the final version. No more laborious re-typing of entire pages on my typewriter. Instead of tediously searching through thick files, I can retrieve old articles from my hard drive or diskettes. My personal computer has made me more efficient and productive.

But you must make your own decision. Consult a reputable dealer and have clearly in mind exactly what you want your computer to do for you. You can save a lot of money by focusing on this and bypassing unnecessary software and technical refinements. Why blow your budget on a BMW when a Holden Barina will get you where you want just as well and far more cheaply? And, just as with a car, you do not need to know the details of how and why it works—you just want to be able to get it up and running.

COMPUTER TALK

'Do I need a computer for my home business?'

If the answer is '*yes*', work through the following checklist.

1. What do I want the computer to do/what applications do I need for my home business?
2. Decide on the software—the computer programs you need. (This may dictate your choice of hardware—Apple, IBM or IBM-compatible.)
3. Decide on the hardware—the mechanical and electrical parts of the computer; the actual computer.
4. Decide on the printer—dot matrix, ink jet or bubble, or laser printer.

   When selecting software, hardware and the printer, consider *price* and *performance.* Balance this against your *budget* and your *work requirements.*
5. Do I want to rent, lease or buy? Which is the best financial option for you, which choice allows you to upgrade? Speak to your accountant about tax deductions and the best option for you.

COMPUTER TIPS

1. Do your research *before* you go to the store. Beware of the computer salesman who steers you towards top-of-the-range technology just for the sake of it. Will you ever make use of this in your home business? Look for a salesperson interested in your requirements.
2. Familiarise yourself by reading computer books, magazines and newspaper articles such as the *Computers and High Technology* section in Tuesday's *Australian* newspaper.
3. Be wary of what your best friend and neighbour have told or shown you. The needs for your home business may be very different.
4. Consider attending a basic computer course, run by local colleges or computer stores.

Filing cabinets

These provide valuable storage space and can fit unobtrusively beneath your desk or in a corner of the room. Do check that, once they are in position, you can fully open the door of your office! Filing cabinets come in two-, three- and four-drawer sizes. A two-drawer filing cabinet costs about $160, compared with $240 for a four-drawer one. 'I often have people come back and say they wished they had bought a larger filing cabinet in the first place,' says Terry Black. 'The space is soon filled up, especially now that people are required to keep five years' worth of tax records.' A four-drawer filing cabinet also lets you avoid stooping—until you fill the lower drawers. With a two-drawer unit, you constantly have to bend down to retrieve and file documents.

Buy new filing cabinets if you can. Second-hand ones may be chipped or battered and come with no warranty. They can cost $180 to $200, so how much are you really saving? If interior frames are missing, it will cost around $7 per drawer to replace them so you can use suspension folders. Most people use metal filing cabinets, which come in a selection of office colours—grey, white, pastel—with a five-year guarantee. If you are going for a smarter look, you may consider laminated board or timber laminate filing cabinets. The former are about $40 dearer than metal filing cabinets, while the latter can cost hundreds of dollars. Examine the runners on any filing cabinet. The more there are, the more the carrying capacity and the longer the cabinet will last, as paper is heavy!

If it is space you are after, metal filing cabinets give the best value for money with about 55 mm more storage room per drawer than other types. You will also need to buy suspension folders—about $25 for a box of 50.

Don't imagine that filing cabinets are either secure or fireproof. 'They will keep out honest people,' says Terry, 'but others will jemmy off the front of the cabinet if they want to get into it.' Though metal filing cabinets may be a little safer in a fire than wooden ones, they will not protect the paper inside from charring. If in doubt, do not store valuable and sensitive material in your filing cabinet. For full protection from fire, you will need an $800 Chubb cabinet.

All in one

Cut down on the decisions and the gadgets by combining them. These days, you can get a telephone, answering machine, fax and photocopier all in one unit. This may suit your present needs, but bear in mind that the combined fax machine and telephone means only one can be used at any one time, and that if one component breaks down, you will have to do without them all while the unit is repaired. Note also that the photocopying facility on the fax machine uses light-sensitive paper and so is unsuitable for copies you want to keep long term.

The work system

You will find you work more efficiently and comfortably if you have a short task break every 30 minutes. If you know a particular job will take you an hour, propose to pause halfway. When working at the computer or sitting for long periods of time, aim to take a regular task break. Ergonomist Jeffrey Frith says that, 'you should not spend more than 50 per cent of your time at the computer, so as to limit the risk of occupational overuse syndrome. Keep your work varied. Alternate time at the computer with paperwork, making telephone calls, filing.'

When you sit, your circulation slows down. Your body weight compresses your muscles, making it harder for the blood to circulate. Compare it to folding a hose to restrict the flow—the water can still get through, but not so efficiently. So get up every half hour—restore the circulation! Stand up and stretch. Breathe in and out deeply. Have a tea break. Listen to a music track. Take a short walk in the garden. You will find your work tolerance dramatically improves after a break of just a few minutes.

When your eyes are fixed at the same focal length—as when working on the computer or reading—they can get strained. So take a minute now and then to *exercise your eyes.* Look at a poster on the wall or look out of the window. Gazing into the distance alters the focal length of your eye muscles and relaxes them.

Listen to your body. Pain is a sign that something is wrong. Do not ignore it. If your neck, arms or shoulders feel sore while you are working, stop and consider why. Perhaps your chair or work position needs to be adjusted. Physiotherapists are used to seeing and treating the kinds of aches and pains that result when people set up a computer on a spare table or sit on a kitchen chair in their home office. Such problems are almost invariably related to posture and, while treatment will relieve the symptoms, prevention is vital. Do not work too long in one position or with your desk or chair at the wrong height.

Rather than spending an entire day each month preparing and sending out invoices, avoid the inevitable stiff back by doing a little each day over a week. Alternatively, break up the task into a series of smaller ones—fold accounts in batches, then put them into envelopes and seal them, rather than doing all this at once.

REVIEW

When setting up your home office, consider:

- location: have a dedicated, separate area if possible
- contents: work through the office equipment checklist on page 55. Decide whether to rent, lease or buy
- design and layout
- ergonomics: short frequent breaks are better than longer infrequent ones. Changes in posture reduce fatigue. Take short walks and breathe fresh air to stimulate your creativity

AN OUTDOOR LIFE

As a tree-surgeon, Piers Laverty does most of his work outdoors. He assesses trees for council development applications, chops down trees in backyards, is involved in tree maintenance and does some pruning, thinning and transplanting. 'I've had an office at home for twelve years and this makes it a lot easier for me as many calls come out of hours,' he says. 'I can respond to them at once. In my line of business, if you can't do that people will go elsewhere.' He lives at Wahroonga, on Sydney's north shore, which he describes as a good central location for his business.

'There was a big storm five years ago and I worked from 5.30 a.m. until midnight for seven weeks, with one day off in that time. It was good for business but I had to take a long break afterwards to recover. Unless I physically go away, I never seem to be able to get away from work. It follows me home, and work and leisure time get blurred.'

Piers has three main pieces of advice for people working from home. 'The first is to separate your life and your work; that is most important. The second is to make sure you have time for yourself and time to think about what you are doing. The third is to keep on top of everything, including the paperwork.'

Running his own business comes naturally to Piers. 'I have never been one for taking orders or carrying out the instructions of others,' he says. 'It is a personality thing—I have always been an intolerant person. I have always been self-employed.'

His line of work, like many others, is becoming more competitive. He tries to counteract this by choosing his jobs carefully—'some are not worth doing'—and building up a pool of regular customers for jobs such as seasonal pruning. 'I used to advertise in the local paper but no longer do so. Inexperienced people will undercut your prices drastically—and then muck up the job. So now I just advertise in the *Yellow Pages* telephone directory and that has been very successful for me.

'The beauty of my type of work is that initially there is

no big capital investment—I need a chainsaw, ute and climbing gear, and I subcontract a lot of work. It can be an intrusive life, with blokes coming round at seven in the morning to pick up gear. I have built a big garage workshop and have found that makes a big difference.

'And I get away whenever I can—I was out kayaking when you called, and picked up your message from my pager.'

ROOM WITH A VIEW

As visual artists, Agnieszka Golda and her husband Martin Johnson find nothing unusual in working from home. 'Artists are traditionally self-employed and cost would be a big factor in renting an outside studio,' they say. 'We are always trying to do things cheaply and simply.'

The couple, who are in their late twenties, have lived and studied in Victoria and South Australia. Agnieszka was able to paint in the spare bedroom of their upstairs Melbourne apartment, but the neighbours complained when Martin took to his wood sculpting with a hammer and chisel. 'It took us three days in a paddock with a handsaw to obtain the log, and now the entire flat was vibrating as Martin worked on it,' says Agnieszka. He was banished to a corner of the downstairs garage but the noise still echoed from there. There was relief all round when the couple moved to Adelaide.

They now live in a large detached cottage on the outskirts of the city. 'The location is ideal,' says Martin, 'just a few minutes' drive from town, and close to Port Adelaide from where I obtain recycled wood.'

They also enjoy the peace and quiet. 'If you can create a relaxing atmosphere around you, you will produce work a lot more easily,' says Agnieszka. 'In the hustle and bustle of the city, you can get easily stressed. This is a peaceful suburb and we have a large garden, with a bench on which I place my paintings to dry. My philosophy is, Create your own environment to feel inspired.'

That inspiration is reflected in their home furnishings:

brightly coloured life-size wooden sculptures fill the large rooms, enormous canvases adorn the walls of the central passage, cushions, tablecloths and a quilt decorated with Agnieszka's textile designs add more colour and warmth. She has an entire room set aside for her art, while Martin has converted a vast area with a concrete floor at the back of the house into his studio. They intend, with council permission, to extend this into the ample back garden.

For Martin and Agnieszka, the advantages of being home-based include the ability to focus on their work, at their own pace, without distractions; the freedom of work hours; and the unregimented lifestyle. Agnieszka likes to work late into the night, while Martin is an early riser. A home studio gives more flexibility than a rented studio with set hours of use. 'You don't have to worry about the noise you are making or about fitting in with the needs of others,' says Martin. 'I'm healthier, and save time and money being home-based—I'll cook curries or goulash for lunch that will last a few days.'

Passionate about their art, this couple never find motivation a problem: they have a focus—perhaps working towards an exhibition—and a daily plan. They set themselves goals, and a time frame in which to achieve those goals. And they make sure they keep a balance between work and leisure. 'We aim to have regular exhibitions,' says Agnieszka. 'As emerging artists, we are aware that it can take years to get a reputation, so we keep costs down as much as possible—making our own frames and stretching our own canvases.'

They have already had several solo exhibitions, and have regular showings at a South Australian gallery. Other income comes from commissions—one of Martin's paintings has been reproduced on a Peter Lehmann wine label—and part-time work—Agnieszka sometimes teaches textile design to students. 'We are not looking for regular part-time work, as this would take us away from our art,' Martin says.

'We have had to make sacrifices but we have chosen to do so,' Agnieszka concedes. 'We don't eat out or go to movies and the car is an old bomb. I buy my clothes at op shops—that can be interesting and unusual. Now I wonder whether I would go to an expensive boutique if I had the money, I'm not used to spending more than $1.20 on a jacket!'

For couples living and working together, Agnieszka and Martin offer these tips: keep your personal and professional lives separate; respect your partner and be supportive; be open and truthful with one another; and pursue your own interests. Each of them has their own style and approach to their work and both say that any competition between them is healthy. 'We are one another's best friends and have found that working from home has brought us closer together.'

4

MONEY MATTERS

Michael Pope was content. Business was going well. Orders for his pottery vases were flooding in from local stores and markets, and he was never short of work. Although he was putting in long hours, he was enjoying the satisfaction of being his own boss and using his artistic skills. He was happy and fulfilled—until he came to look at his earnings.

After Michael had paid for his materials, other bills such as gas, electricity and telephone, and living expenses—food and rent—he was left with very little indeed. 'It's just not worth it,' he grumbled. 'I would have been better off sticking with my clerical job.' But he decided to give his business another go. He doubled the price of his vases. 'That will give me a reasonable income,' he told himself.

Suddenly demand dropped. Few of his customers were prepared to pay the new price. Those who were asked if they could pay in instalments, and Michael readily agreed. Yet, all at once, he had far fewer customers but just as many bills. Bills that he was no longer able to pay.

Where did Michael go wrong?

In several areas. He had not prepared a business plan at the outset and he had not done any research into costing. Instead, he had simply set a price that he thought the stores and markets would pay. He had not calculated the cost of his materials and his labour. Nor had he looked at what his competitors were charging, what similar vases were fetching or what people were prepared to pay. Then, by suddenly doubling the price of his product, he effectively put himself out of business. By far Michael's gravest mistake was that he ignored the importance of cash flow. He had to learn the hard way that *a business can survive without profits, but it cannot survive without cash flow.*

What should Michael have done to keep his business in the black and avoid a return to paper shuffling? First, he should have looked more closely at costing from the start. After calculating what his materials and labour were worth, he could have added a 25 per cent profit margin and checked to see whether his clients would pay the total amount. This would have prevented his having to extend credit to his customers and ensured that when the bills came in, he had the cash to pay them. He could also have diversified into other products—smaller vases, mugs or plates which did not take as long to make and would have generated more profit.

Carried away with the prospect of doing what he loved for a living, Michael failed to look closely enough at how his passion for pottery could provide him with an adequate, and even a comfortable, living. He did not study in-depth the economics of his venture.

Kate McLauchlan was eager to get going with her typing and writing business. She gave notice to her employer and, over the next month, she set up a home office, leased a computer and printer, bought a fax and answering machine, and stocked up on office supplies. Unlike Michael, she was successful from the outset. Her previous employer was happy to supply her with work and recommend her to others. Friends and acquaintances made good use of her quick and efficient, high-quality and well-priced service.

Before going into business for herself, Kate had accurately assessed the likely demand for her services. She had built up a list of prospective clients and had priced her services at a level that was within the market range and also provided her with a reasonable profit. She had also taken into account that her income might be low at first, as the business found its feet, so she made sure she had savings to back her up for the first few months. Like Michael, Kate was happy and fulfilled—until the time came to fill in her tax return. Her accountant's words filled her with dismay. She faced a tax bill of over $14,000.

How on earth would she be able to pay it? She only had $3,000 in savings. She had put some of her profits back into the business and spent other money on clothes and holidays. Kate had not frittered her money away but neither had she prepared herself for this eventuality. And now, like Michael, she had put herself out of business. Unlike Michael, though, she had done very well in her two years of trading. However, had Kate consulted an accountant earlier, she would still be in business. For the accountant would have explained to her the concept of provisional tax. She would have been advised to put money aside in a separate account to prepare for it and told about possible tax deductions. Because a computer can be depreciated for tax purposes at 50 per cent a year, for example, she would have been better off buying rather than leasing the computer and leasing, rather than buying, the fax machine.

Seeing the accountant early could have saved Kate's business. The point here is that it makes sense to see an accountant *before* you go into business.

Before you start

See an accountant!

Adelaide accountant Jamie McKeogh is talking about the many would-be small businesspeople who have consulted him. 'They come in all keen and leave shattered and reconsidering their decision.' After an hour with Jamie, people are left with a lot to consider.

Jamie is not pessimistic, just realistic. 'Many people have a false impression of being in business,' he says. 'It is a huge amount of hard work, and you need to ask yourself whether you are ready to handle the pressures. There is a big difference between running your own business and working for someone else.'

An accountant such as Jamie will help you look at the many legal, financial and managerial aspects involved in setting up your own business, home-based or not. He'll tell you about the need to keep records, do bookkeeping, and prepare financial statements and tax returns. He'll give you information about registering a business name. If you are buying an established business, your accountant can look at the past business records and recommend on whether this is likely to be a good decision or not. He can also advise on franchises. If you employ someone else, he can organise such things as group tax and superannuation payments. He can help you decide on your business's structure: whether it should be a sole trader, a partnership, a limited liability company or a trust (see Chapter 2). This is important, because if your business booms after a year and you decide to change its structure, the transfer might include capital gains tax and stamp duty and could cost you big dollars.

An hour with an accountant, assessing whether your home-based business is a practical proposition, is an hour well spent. It will cost you between $100 and $170 but how much better to pay $170 now than to pay hundreds more for him to sort out your mess later! And, as the saying goes, 'Don't be afraid to ask dumb questions. They're easier to handle than dumb mistakes.'

Getting your business going

Angela Basso was seeking a loan of $10,000 to get her home-based catering business established. She wanted to upgrade her oven and install an exhaust fan. She needed food processors, bigger and better-quality saucepans, and other kitchen utensils. Having itemised and priced the articles she required, she confidently approached her bank manager.

> 'A new business?' he asked. 'Tell me more.'
> Angela looked puzzled. 'What would you like to know?'
> 'Have you made out a business plan?'
> 'No.'
> 'Have you had experience in catering?'
> 'Well . . . not on this scale.'

The bank manager looked again at the information Angela had presented to him. 'You have had an account with us for many years,' he said. 'You are a good customer. But we need to know a lot more than this so we will feel comfortable lending you the money.'

'I am convinced my business will go really well,' enthused Angela. 'I already have a lot of companies interested in me supplying them with boardroom lunches and . . .'

'How much profit will you be making?' interrupted the bank manager.

'I don't know exactly.'

'You might not make any,' explained the bank manager. 'In that case, how will you be able to repay the loan? And what will you live on, if you don't make any money?'

'At least I can eat the food,' chuckled Angela.

But the bank manager had the last laugh, for she did not get her loan.

You may think that Angela was naive and ill-prepared. She was. This was her first attempt at business. Now, ten years on, and the owner of a successful business, she knows better. But she learned the hard way—from overcoming avoidable setbacks and embarrassments along the way.

Meanwhile, wetsuit manufacturer Roy Williams had no trouble obtaining finance to set up his home business. His detailed and comprehensive business plan, coupled with his previous experience in the area, stood him in good stead. He impressed the bank manager so much with his knowledge, written information and confidence that the bank actually offered him *more* than he was asking for!

Start-up capital

Loans can be obtained from banks, credit unions or other financial institutions. Perhaps you do not need one and can make do with your own savings or money borrowed from family members. Maybe you do not expect to have big initial outlays. But *make absolutely sure you have enough start-up capital.* Underestimating capital needs is one of the most common reasons for small business failure.

A loan is appropriate when you wish to purchase business equipment and pay off the whole amount. You borrow a certain amount of money, at an agreed interest rate, for a set number of years. But if you expect your bank balance to fluctuate when funding debtors or buying stock—if you need working capital—an overdraft is more appropriate. In its most straightforward form, this is an agreement with your bank on an amount by which you may overdraw your account for a set period. Interest may be calculated on the size of the overdraft.

How does a home-based business obtain a loan?

The fact that a business is home-based is not significant, says Canberra bank manager Maria Costas. What banks look at is the viability of the business, the background of the person going into it and how he or she is going to be able to repay the loan. They want to look at a solid business plan and forecasts of the capacity to repay the loan.

Previous experience in the same business is an advantage. It would be very difficult for someone to get a loan for a computer consultancy business if they had previously sold vegetables all their life. The bank would not look upon this situation favourably and would have severe doubts as to whether they could make the business work. But if their previous employment had revolved around computers, the bank would be far more likely to approve their loan.

You have to convince your bank manager that you are capable, knowledgeable and experienced. If you have not previously worked in the field, you must be able to demonstrate that you are aware of sound business principles and practices, that you have carried out sufficient research into your proposed enterprise, and that you are thoroughly prepared.

It is far easier for the bank to approve a loan if you have proven business acumen. They look at past financial statements and consider income, sales and expenditure forecasts for the new business. They want you to be able to demonstrate a capacity to repay the finance, and need sound information to give you good banking advice.

When a person is starting in business for the first time, the bank is more cautious. Most people have a bit of a 'pie in the sky' attitude and find it hard to make realistic forecasts. But if you have contracts in place and a guaranteed income, that will impress the bank. A business plan will also go in your favour. *These* are the requirements for success. The last thing the bank looks at is the security for the loan—shares, insurance policies, mortgage equity.

Another way of obtaining start-up capital is by way of a business grant. This enabled Adelaide draftsman Peter Robertson to get started (see page 47). Having been laid off from his job with the Housing Trust Peter attempted to work for himself but was unable to make sufficient income. 'I had to register for social security and ended up with lots of messy paperwork and very little money,' he says. 'This was because I was continually going on and off the dole as jobs came in.' He continued in this unsatisfactory manner until a friend told him of the federal government's New Enterprise Incentive Scheme, NEIS, set up to provide small business management training, advice and a year's income support for unemployed people wishing to set up their own business.

Peter fulfilled the eligibility criteria of being unemployed and registered with the CES for full-time work, and was accepted into the intensive six-week NEIS course. After preparing a business plan which was approved by the NEIS board, he was provided with a business mentor and fortnightly payments over a year, while his design drafting business became established. 'The amount was exactly the same as the dole,' he says, 'but since I was allowed to keep it all, in addition to my drafting income, I was able to get my business going.'

Had it not been for NEIS, it is unlikely that Peter would have been able to run his own business. His story shows how worthwhile it can be to look at all options available to you.

Up and running

You are in business to make a living, so your prices are crucial. Charge too much and no one will buy. Charge too little and you will soon be out of pocket—and business. The secret is to strike a balance between what the market can bear and what you need to live on.

How to set costs

The same principles apply whether you are pricing a product or a service. You need to strike a balance between the market rate and your proposed income.

When organisational psychologist Bruce Crowe started his home business, he checked with his professional body and with other practitioners offering similar services to determine the recommended hourly rate and what others were charging. He now had a guide on which to base his own fees.

Once Bruce had an idea of the rate he could charge, he looked at his ongoing costs, such as living expenses and mortgage repayments. He looked at how many clients he could realistically expect. And he determined on making a profit of 25 per cent. On this basis he was able to fine-tune his fee.

Another way to approach this calculation is to ask yourself how much you would like to make in a year. Now ask yourself how many hours a week you are prepared to work for that income. For the sake of simplicity, let us say you wish to earn $50,000 a year and you want two weeks' holiday. You intend to work 40 hours a week, that is 2,000 hours a year. Therefore you will need to charge $25 an hour. There are other factors to consider. Is there enough work for you to be able to work 40 hours a week? Are you allowing yourself any leeway—for time lost due to illness, family commitments or other things? Are you being realistic, or overly optimistic? Of the 40 hours a week you intend to work, are all of those hours *chargeable* time? No, of course not. Do not forget this vital point!

At a conservative estimate, only 50 to 60 per cent of your time is chargeable. Look at 30 per cent being administration time for your business. 'The rest is "wandering around" time for me,' says Bruce Crowe. 'I spend that doing things such as perusing professional journals and contributing to my professional associations.'

So your year contains, at best, 1,200 chargeable hours. To earn that $50,000, you will need to charge your clients in the order of $41 an hour. Is this feasible? If not, will you settle for a lower income or, alternatively, put in more hours?

This can be a very valuable exercise. Once you have estimated what your time is worth, you can set about improving the turnover of your business. If your time is charged at $30 an hour, for example, it is far more economical for you to use a courier, at the cost of about $7, to deliver a package to a client than to spend an hour or more taking it yourself. Invest that hour in your business, earn $30 and be $23 ahead.

Better still, the courier charge is tax deductible as a legitimate business expense.

Making fees work for you

Your business is up and running and you have no shortage of clients—among them many friends and acquaintances. Yet there are unexpected problems.

'Initially, I found it hard to ask for money,' says homoeopath Meredith Norman. 'I think this is a problem for many women. We tend to undervalue ourselves. It was difficult for me to set a realistic charge and to stick to it. I made concessions for friends when there was no need to do so. They certainly did not expect it and, looking at it realistically, they did not need it either, as they earned more than I did! This was *my* problem and not theirs.'

Meredith learnt to change her ways. 'I got a shock at tax time when I looked at my income. It was much lower than I had thought.' So now she does 'no more favours for friends. It is fine to make allowances for people in need, but I now know I have to strike a balance between providing a service that is accessible to a good number of people and one that provides me with a decent income. Otherwise it is pointless. I learnt the hard way but, even now, I tend to err on the generous side. I occasionally give a client a remedy free of charge.'

Jan Sutherland, of Dial-A-Wife cleaning services, was also hesitant about sticking to her fees at first. 'I would give too low a price in case I lost the job. But your confidence grows with the business. Now I am selective and say we give a quality service. I am no longer prepared to compromise.' Besides, she says, 'People do not value the service if you do not charge properly'.

Jan's and Meredith's message is: *Set realistic charges and stick to them.*

Working from home can mean lower overheads, a saving you can pass on to your clients in the form of *competitive fees*. That's what interior designer Catherine Bugoss and her partner do. 'Our fee structure is based on our years of experience, the guidelines of the Design Institute of Australia, and the nature of the project—whether it is domestic or commercial,' explains Catherine. 'Our fees are less than those charged by interior designers working in city offices. To us, that is the whole point of working from home—you can offer the same amount of experience and the same quality of work for less money.' They draw attention to this in their glossy prospectus: 'Not bogged down with high overheads or unwieldy corporate structures, we are flexible, responsive, efficient, and our fees are moderate.' Their approach works. Their tenders have been accepted over those of much larger companies.

Managing money

How is it that some people on high salaries are constantly struggling financially while others do very well on much less? The answer lies not in the *size* of the salary but in how it is *managed.*

If you cannot trust yourself with *credit cards*, avoid them. 'I have paid off my credit-card debts and destroyed the cards,' says computer consultant Wesley Brown. 'I have no debts and I have a healthy bank balance.' An enviable position to be in, yet Wesley had to work hard to get there. 'Credit cards can be a big trap,' he says. 'You can easily use them to spend beyond your means. And the interest rate on them is very high.' Wesley took out a personal loan at a low variable interest rate to pay off his credit-card debts. 'Afterwards I cut the cards up with scissors and set about paying off the personal loan.'

Your *books must be kept in good order*, both to run your business efficiently and for tax purposes. Your accountant can advise you on what records need to be kept and small business courses and books will show you how. If you don't savour the prospect of bookkeeping, employ a professional to do it for you on a regular basis. This can save you much frustration and time you would be better off putting into your work.

Naturally, you'll be concerned if your customers don't settle their accounts promptly, so make sure you settle your own accounts on time. It helps to budget for regular bills. 'I put money aside every week for gas and electricity expenses,' says

Wesley Brown, 'so that when the quarterly bill arrives, I am ahead.'

Dealing with debtors

As with illness, so with debts: *Prevention is better than cure.* In the most extreme case, bad debts can cripple and even kill your business. Consider this. If your profit margin is 10 per cent, you will need to generate *$1,000* in sales to recoup that *$100* owed to you. Even if you manage to collect the $100 from your debtor two months down the track, it may now be worth only $90 or less because of the work time you've lost in collecting it. Clearly, it makes sense to steer clear of bad debts altogether. But how?

You need to exercise trust and tact in dealing with customers. But there can be a fine line between trusting your customer and protecting yourself. Here are some recommendations to bear in mind:

1. Inform your customers about your trading terms at the outset

Tell them clearly and state on your invoice that payment is due immediately or after seven, fourteen or 30 days. Send out your invoices promptly.

2. Have a credit limit

The way to work out this limit is simple. Ask yourself *'How much can I afford to lose?'* If you can deliver your product C.O.D.—cash on delivery—do so. If you must give credit, insist on a few C.O.D. transactions first before letting your customer apply for a 30-day account. Ask your solicitor to help you draw up the application form. It should ask the customer to supply personal guarantees and trade references and demonstrate an ability to pay. Naturally, such measures are only necessary when large sums of money are involved.

3. Keep an eye on where things are going

Be aware of late payments and be prepared to go after them. Make sure your books are *always* up to date. Write everything down, don't try to keep it all in your head. Once you put it on paper, you may discover the situation is not as benign as you thought.

4. Remind the customer early

Businesses often run into trouble because their owners do not ask for help soon enough. If you have not received payment by the due date, remind your customer with a friendly telephone call. There may be a reasonable explanation—he may have genuinely forgotten. Should you feel uncomfortable making such a telephone call, ask someone else—who can do so confidently—to make it on your behalf.

5. Move swiftly

The longer you wait before taking action, the more difficult it can be to obtain payment. If the account has not been settled within a week of contacting your renegade customer, send out a letter requesting payment. Follow this up with two more letters seven days apart. Turn up the severity. Tell the customer that you will take legal action if you do not receive payment in full.

For outstanding debts less than a certain amount (which varies from state to state), you can take the customer to a small claims court. Only you can decide whether it is worth the time, hassle and (minimal) expense. Even if you win the case, if your customer says he is in financial difficulty, he may be ordered to repay the debt in small weekly instalments. Worse still, if he should fail to do so, it is up to you to pursue the matter—and take him back to court.

Another possibility is to contract a debt collector or credit controller to act on your behalf. Naturally you will have to pay for this service, so, depending on the size of the debt, you will have to decide whether it's worth taking action. Bear in mind that debt collectors have more difficulty collecting a payment that is two months overdue than with one that is just a few days late.

Many bad debts can be nipped in the bud if you pay attention to some key warning signs:

1. Rumours

Keep your eyes and ears open. Keep in contact with the other suppliers or workers in your area. If you hear that a certain customer is having trouble paying his bills, don't accept large orders from him.

2. Request for credit

If someone who has previously dealt with your competition suddenly approaches you and asks for credit, ask yourself why. Perhaps he has been refused goods or services by the other businesses because of non-payment. Again, it is wise to keep your ear to the ground.

3. Large orders or payment in instalments

If a customer who has previously paid promptly unexpectedly builds up a large account or asks to pay in instalments, he may be having cash-flow problems. Tread warily.

4. Non-payment

If a customer abruptly defaults on a regular payment, this could also signal trouble, especially if the customer is always unavailable when you call and does not return your messages. Delaying tactics, such as the customer's wrongfully claiming he did not get your invoice or was dissatisfied with the work or products, are another warning sign.

In all these cases, remember it is the squeaky hinge that gets oiled—so get in first! On the other hand, be prepared to make allowances for previously reliable or longstanding customers. If they are in temporary difficulty, dealing with the problem amiably and patiently can be beneficial for both parties. Be neither overly suspicious nor too relaxed. Where you believe you have genuine concerns about whether the debt will be paid, *act promptly*!

Jan and Ross Sutherland of Dial-A-Wife cleaning services avoid bad debts by obtaining payment upfront wherever possible. 'It is not a problem for us,' says Jan. 'We usually get cash on completion of a cleaning job. The client will leave the money, or a cheque, in an envelope. Otherwise we will invoice them and the next time we clean, they pay. We do not carry debts for any length of time. The only clients we have to wait on are builders. They are notorious for making late payments anyway, but they are not a major source of our income.'

Architect Wayne Ketchen also refuses to carry bad debts. 'My invoice makes my terms clear,' he says. 'Payment is due within fourteen days. After that time I send a follow-up letter with a copy of the invoice, and a cover note saying "In case this slipped your mind . . ." I then make a polite telephone call to the client about another matter, and mention the bill. This tends to work pretty well.'

TALKING TAX

A home business is just like any other—whatever you make you have to share it with the tax man. There are important tax planning matters that you should really talk about, early, with your accountant—provisional tax, tax records, the deductions you might claim, whether or not to incorporate a company, etc. It *will* cost you not to talk to your accountant.

When it comes to tax deductions, ask whether you are maintaining a home study or workshop, or running a business from home. A home study is any convenient space where you set up your work. Running a business from home involves having a space that is used exclusively for business purposes, such as a doctor's consulting room or the shed set aside especially for making and marketing your widgets. Spaces that clients come to, but your family usually doesn't.

Maintaining a home office, study or workshop

If you have a home office you can only claim running expenses related to that space. Deductions must be based on the time it is used as an office and can include a proportion of: light and power costs, heating and cooling, telephone expenses, cleaning and maintenance. You may also be able to claim depreciation on furniture and fittings and your professional library.

Running a business from home

If you are truly operating a 'home business' this is likely to be you. As well as the running expenses listed above, you may claim a proportion of the occupancy expenses associated with your whole house—repairs, council and water rates, home and contents insurance, mortgage interest or rent. However, if you sell the house that contains your place of business, you may have to pay a capital gains tax on the sale. Running a business from home may also entitle you to deduct fuller travel expenses.

Ask your accountant for advice and details on all these matters and the records you must keep. Remember that, by law, your tax records need to be kept for five years.

Are you covered?

When Barbara Chandler returned from a weekend in the country to find her unit had been broken into, she was devastated. Her only consolation was that her home-contents insurance policy would cover the stolen computer and printer. But she discovered, to her horror, that this was not the case. To protect your office equipment, or any cash in the office, you need additional cover. In most cases, the extra payment is small. Don't pennypinch here: a robbery can ruin your business.

When looking at insurance, you might consider the various types available.

- *Professional indemnity and product liability* protects you against negligence and injury caused by your product.
- *Public liability* covers you against accidental injury to customers and visitors to your business premises. If one of them trips over the carpet and breaks an ankle, you do not want to be up for thousands of dollars in medical bills.
- *Sickness and disability insurance* protects your income in case you become ill or have a disabling accident. There are many forms of such cover available. Consult an insurance broker or company. It's also advisable to line up another individual or company to take over your projects if you are unable to work for a few days—and vice versa.
- *Superannuation* is no longer a part of your salary package. Now that you are self-employed it is up to you to provide

for your retirement. You may prefer to invest your superannuation savings in real estate rather than a super fund. The choice is yours.

- *Car insurance* is vital for your business vehicle. If you use your private vehicle for the business, you will need to inform your insurer and the policy and premium will be adjusted accordingly.
- *Life insurance* is advisable for everyone involved with the business.
- *Making a will* is not a task most of us like to contemplate. But as we all know, death, like taxes, is inevitable, and without a will, what will happen to your partner, children or other dependents?

REVIEW

A business can survive without profits, but it cannot survive without cash flow.

Before you start

- Consult an accountant
- Get your business structure right from the outset
- If you require start-up capital:
  apply for a loan or overdraft
  apply for a business grant

Up and running

- Set realistic costs for your goods and services
- Prepare for provisional tax by putting money aside in a separate account

Ongoing finances

- Adhere to your costs and charges
- Use your lower fees as a marketing tool
- Budget
- Keep proper records, as advised by your accountant and business courses

Dealing with debtors

Prevention is better than cure

- Make your customers aware of your trading terms at the outset
- Set a credit limit
- Keep a close watch on your business
- Follow up unsettled accounts promptly by telephone calls and with letters
- Act early to recover bad debts
- If necessary, hire a debt collector

Are you covered?

Look at:

- Insurance of house and office contents, including office equipment
- Professional indemnity and product liability
- Public liability
- Sickness and disability insurance
- Superannuation
- Car insurance
- Life insurance
- Making a will

SUITED TO THE JOB

Melbourne-based journalist and desktop publisher Paula Ruzek is pleased with her decision in January 1990 to quit her job with a national business magazine and work for herself from home. 'I'm very suited to this lifestyle,' she says, 'I have the skills and the right mental discipline.'

Specialising in the production of government and professional publications, Paula processes and edits written material, does desktop publishing and layout design, liaises with typesetters and printers, and makes editorial decisions.

Paula used the holiday pay and other money she got on leaving *Business Review Weekly* to purchase the equipment she needed, and launched into full-time work straight away.

'When I started at the *Age* newspaper as a sub-editor in 1984, I worked from 6 p.m. until 1 a.m. That gave me the capacity to freelance during the day and I started picking up regular work.' Freelancing became more difficult once she moved to *Business Review Weekly* four years later. 'This was a day job, from 10 to 6,' she says. 'It showed me the procedure of how to produce a quality publication under deadline pressures. I liked the people I was working with and the environment was great. But the work I was doing was very repetitive and I had no say in the final product. I decided I had all the skills I needed by then to set up on my own.'

She found a large job immediately, by word of mouth, becoming editor of *HRMonthly*, the magazine of the Australian Human Resources Institute which comes out eleven times a year. Other work soon came in. 'As soon as I would start wondering where the next job was coming from, the telephone would ring with an offer.'

The only lean patch was a couple of years later, due to an unexpected tax bill. 'I should have made sure I had put some money away each month,' confesses Paula. 'I had not been keeping track of what I was earning as I thought it would be the same as the previous year.' Fortunately she was able to find casual work back at the *Age* to get her through this financial hiccup. Today Paula has learnt her lesson and keeps a close watch over her income and her expenditure. She says she is now in a better financial position than she would be had she stayed working for an employer.

'I work really hard, day and night for all but a few days of each month, to get *HRMonthly* and the institute's newspaper, *Inside AHRI*, completed. As a freelancer, you have to be really disciplined to be successful—working eight, ten or twelve hours a day to get the job done. You *must* meet deadlines, give the ultimate in customer service and be really client-focused. You can't just sit back and expect someone else on the team to do the work. You can be a total slob in the office but what you present to the client must be of superior quality and presentation. Get the work done *and* on time. Meet and *exceed* client expectations.'

The only downside for Paula, if indeed there is one, comes with the timing of holidays. 'I can really only have a break in December, when the publications I work for do not put out issues. But I don't see that as particularly negative. I knew all of that before I started.'

Paula is bemused when people ask her, as they inevitably do of home-based workers, whether she is lonely. 'Of course I'm not,' she replies. 'I'm being very productive and am not being interrupted by people all the time, wanting to chat. I can make or receive up to 30 work phone calls a day and I have built up great relationships with the people I work with, over the phone. I make sure I get out and see my friends. I'm certainly not lacking in human contact.'

Yet she can understand the qualms of others. 'Working from home is certainly not for everyone,' she says.

MAKING A SPLASH

When Roy Williams and his wife arrived in Australia from England in 1992, he could not find a job. 'I was a wetsuit manufacturer in the UK but there was nothing for me here in Adelaide. I spent a year looking for work, going for four jobs a week. I was prepared to do anything, even sweep the roads, but it was a waste of time. I was considered too old.'

Roy, who has recently turned 61, became despondent. 'I gave up in the end. You might as well dig a hole and bury yourself.' He decided to start his own home business instead but got initial discouragement there also. He was told there were already two or three other wetsuit manufacturers in South Australia and that there was no room for another, but his research had informed him otherwise, and he set out to prove his critics wrong. 'I found a niche in the market,' he says. 'I specialise in made-to-measure suits, not off-the-peg ones.' He does not advertise much—only once a month in the *Trader*, which costs him $10—and he started by making wetsuits for the police and Navy. Word soon spread and the orders came flooding in. 'I had more trade than you could ever imagine,' he says.

The good news continued when the bank he approached was so impressed by his previous experience and his comprehensive business plan that it approved his request for an overdraft and offered him more than he had asked for!

This former diving instructor started in the industry in 1969, in Essex, England. He has made outfits for Sean Connery in the film *Thunderball* and devised thin waterproof outfits for the water-battle scenes in the Robin Hood movie *Prince of Thieves*.

Val, Roy's wife, works as an accountant outside the house. She manages his books 'and keeps us on the right track'. Roy also makes 'dry suits' for professional divers. He works from a shed next to the house in which he has industrial sewing machines. He has council permission and says, 'Gawler council have been absolute diamonds, very helpful'. His nearest neighbour is 200 metres away and the shed backs onto open land.

'I make a reasonable living,' Roy says. 'I'm not here to make myself a millionaire. My business is growing each year, slowly, but I wanted a good foundation. The first year it went up 50 per cent and now it is 75 per cent up. I like being my own governor and I've made a ten-year plan. A little bit of something is better than a big bit of nothing, I say. With big debts, you can crash overnight, so I move very slowly.'

5

PERFORMANCE AND PRESENTATION

Your *professional image* flows through every aspect of your business—from your telephone manner to your stationery, from your personal appearance to the quality and reliability of your work. Many home-business owners have encountered the incorrect but widely held belief that a home-based business is inferior to one located in a city office, for example. Certainly there are 'backyarders', just as there are shonky businesspeople in every field. Yet the majority of those working in home-based businesses do so from choice rather than necessity, and consequently are very committed to their venture. They are, after all, directly and personally responsible for their goods and services and derive great satisfaction from this. With lower overheads, they are usually able to offer very competitive prices, and they must also offer quality as good as, if not better than, their competitors do in order to survive.

People are keen to work from home for many reasons—convenience, savings in rent, autonomy—yet they are not so keen to make this fact public. Children's book illustrator Craig Smith (see page 136) admits, 'I don't broadcast the fact that

I work from home. I say "office premises" or put it in similar terms. The reason is that I am sensitive to the bedroom image some people have of home-based workers.' It's an inaccurate image, he agrees. This false view of home workers 'is not a big concern to me, but I am aware of it'.

Interior designer Catherine Bugoss believes she and her partner have lost out on some contracts by being home-based. 'Many organisations still have the idea that people who work from home are not serious,' she says. 'Clients will say, "you don't have a secretary or an infrastructure? We don't think you can handle a big job." Yet we know we *can*. We point out that we can call on other resources and that our overheads are lower precisely because we do *not* have a large infrastructure.'

Far from being unable to do the work requested of them, Catherine and her partner may in fact be better suited to it. They know many interior designers and can call upon the most appropriate for each job. 'In this way, we have greater scope than a company with the same employees all the time,' says Catherine. 'Things will change, it just takes time. We think that, in the next two years, corporate clients will accept businesses working from home.'

Catherine and her partner have much more success conveying a professional image through their striking colour brochure. They know that *a professional image is vital when it comes to finding and generating work and developing repeat business.*

Have you ever been treated rudely or inconsiderately by a shop assistant or tradesperson? Did you give that person the benefit of the doubt, thinking, 'Oh, he is just having a bad day'? Probably not. More likely, you decided that the store or company offered lousy service and resolved to avoid dealing with it again. And you probably told your friends and acquaintances about your experience, warning them to steer clear.

Have you ever been let down by the late delivery of a product or by a faulty item or service and, when you complained, been treated politely, efficiently and with respect? If your money has been refunded or the product exchanged—promptly, with an apology and with little fuss—has your confidence not been completely restored? Did you tell your friends about it? Probably not. Somehow bad service seems to make a far better story than good.

It has been said that every dissatisfied client will tell seventeen others while a satisfied one will only tell three or four—a point well worth keeping in mind in your own business.

The point is that *you* represent your company. You aren't just Jean Duncan but Jean Duncan Designs. You are Norwood Accountants as well as Roger and Jane Wilson. So building up a good reputation depends on you and you alone. And this crucial process starts with your first contact with the customer.

Telephone technique

For most people, that first contact is by phone, so your telephone manner is extremely important. Follow these guidelines:

- Identify yourself with your business name
- Speak clearly, brightly and confidently
- Be polite and helpful at all times
- Avoid distracting background sounds—music playing, children screaming
- Give the caller your complete attention—do not shuffle through papers, eat, drink or smoke while speaking. The caller may not be able to see you do this but can certainly *hear* you
- Train others in the household to answer the telephone correctly or else warn them against doing so. Nothing will give your business a worse image than a child's voice saying, 'Dad's not here and I don't know when he'll be back'
- Never argue with a customer. Listen to her complaint. The relief of talking may be sufficient to defuse her anger. The customer is always right
- If you have an *answering machine*, record a new message regularly. The change of a few words or a slightly different tone in your voice will make a favourable impression on regular callers, who know your old message word for word. Keep your message brief, serious and to the point. There was a fad at one time for humorous messages. It may be mildly amusing for some to learn that you are unavailable

as you are 'in the shower with a blonde', but the novelty soon wears off. There is nothing more irritating than 'clever' or music-embellished messages, especially if you have to hear them more than once. One thing that does work, however, is using your answering machine as a marketing tool. Marilyn Jolly uses her telephone message to give the caller brief details of her home and pet care services. So, while Marilyn may be unavailable to answer any queries at the time, the caller can gain useful information from the message

For Julie and Andrew Matthews, whose Cairns company markets Andrew's talks, seminars and books—the million-selling *Being Happy*, *Making Friends*, *Get Faxed!* and *Follow Your Heart*—making a bad impression on the phone 'can cost you your speaking engagement and your reputation'. With this in mind, Julie has typed out a couple of scripts to help their secretary answer the telephone proficiently.

'When you make a call, I think it is important to say who you are up front: "This is Julie calling from Andrew Matthews Productions." The other person does not then have to ask who you are or where you are calling from. It is also a very confident and assertive thing to do.'

Making words work

Whether you are sending a letter to a prospective client, mailing out a brochure or making a letterbox drop of leaflets advertising your services, professionalism is imperative.

Your words and presentation reflect the image and competence of your business. Make sure they do not let you down. Check the grammar and spelling. Have the layout designed by experts. Use the form that is most appropriate for you in terms of cost and effectiveness.

You may choose to make up a full-colour brochure with details and photographs of your work experience. Interior designer Catherine Bugoss and her partner place this information in an attractive blue matt folder embossed with their business logo, and post it to prospective clients. This is an expense for which they have budgeted, and it has been money well spent, for it has helped them attract good clients and big projects.

Marilyn Jolly, who does not do such lucrative one-off projects, has had simple but effective two-colour leaflets printed, with details of her home and pet care services. She places these in pet shops and veterinary surgeries in her area.

Julie Matthews feels very strongly about printed material. 'Your business card is *you*,' she says. 'It portrays how you feel about yourself, how big or small-time you are, how confident you are. It is a pity some people make their telephone number and address so small you can't see them. They should be prominent. You must be prepared to spend money on good-quality paper and printing so that people will hold onto your card.' Naturally, the scale of this depends on your type of business, your budget and what is appropriate. The business card for Andrew Matthews Productions folds out into three sections, is in full colour and lists Andrew's services as well as contact details.

'When you hand over your card, the person receiving it must be impressed,' Julie believes. 'He will instantly make up his mind about you, your business and your product. You need to show that you are not cheap.'

Andrew Matthews' card is geared towards his particular market and clientele. An individual or business with a lower profile and looking for small contracts can still pack a punch with a simple, inexpensive business card. Make your business cards appropriate—a window cleaner may not need as elaborate a card as a lawyer does, although you never know—this could be a good advertising gimmick! Whatever the case, it usually pays to have your card professionally designed. Avoid the vending machines that offer on-the-spot business cards for a few dollars. Cheap, flimsy cards convey the image that your business also provides a cheap, trashy service.

But don't waste money on overly colourful or gimmicky cards, either. 'I had some really nice business cards made up when I started Your Type Secretarial Services,' says Jenny Church. 'Many people tend to get lovely letterhead stationery and business cards printed when they start up—it is a psychological boost. But it is also an extravagance, at a time when you can least afford it. Business cards can be expensive.'

The simplest design or logo can still be effective and sophisticated. Good design is the key. Do not clutter the card with too much information—this just looks amateurish and can be difficult to read. Stick to the essentials—name and qualifications, address, telephone, fax, e-mail numbers and goods or services offered. The graphic designer will suggest various designs for you to choose from and perhaps help you coordinate your cards with other business stationery—headed notepaper, leaflets or brochures, compliment slips or fax cover sheets—and with a business logo.

Writer Libby Gleeson's two-tone business card, in deep blue, is complemented by a similar two-tone brochure listing her numerous publications and giving her background and contact details. A photograph of Libby adorns the front cover, together with her name and 'Writer' in the same large italics as on her business card. 'People always comment favourably on my card and brochure,' says Libby. 'A graphic designer worked on them and then I had them printed by a large company. They look better than they should for the cost and I think the secret to that is good design.'

Invoices

There are several ways in which you can save time, money and postage with invoices. Send the original invoice to your client, together with a duplicate. The duplicate can be retained by the client as a receipt, and the original posted back to you with payment. Or you may have a single sheet for your invoice with a detachable lower section to be mailed back with payment.

Make your terms of trading very clear, both to the client and on the invoice. State 'payment is due within seven days'—or whatever is appropriate in your case. For reminders about late payments, Andrew Matthews has an appropriate form in his book *Get Faxed!* This fax form, pictured opposite, vividly illustrates the problems caused by delayed payment.

Post office box

This, too, can be part of your professional image. When you have a postal address, none of the clients you deal with by

Attention: .... Company: ....

Tel: .... Fax: ....

From: .... Company ....

Tel: .... Fax: ....

Account Number .... Amount Owing ....

to order *'GET FAXED!'* in Australia fax 070 576 966

mail or phone need be aware that you work from home. The bonus is added security. No longer can your letters and packages be pilfered by others or drenched by rain. Mail need not be redirected when you are away. It is automatically kept for you at the post office.

By far one of the biggest advantages for those in home-based businesses is that your mail is sorted and placed in your post office box first thing in the morning, so you can deal with it at the start of the day, rather than waiting until late afternoon for it to be delivered to your home.

A post office box can also save you money. Should you move house but remain in the same area, you can keep the same box, stationery and business cards rather than having to print new ones. Prices vary according to the size and location of the box. A small post office box at a suburban post office can cost $40 a year, while a large post office box at the GPO can cost more than $250.

Face-to-face contact

French fashion designer Coco Chanel once said, 'If you dress smartly, they'll remember the dress. But dress impeccably and they'll remember the woman.' Whether you are male or female, appearance is important. As with words, a sloppy look detracts from your overall image. Prospective clients may take the next logical step and assume that your work is also likely to be unkempt or slipshod.

People set great store by first impressions. So why not give yourself the best possible chance? Psychologists say that, on first meeting someone, almost 60 per cent of our attention is occupied with the person's physical appearance, over 30 per cent with their manner and tone of voice, and less than 10 per cent by what he or she is actually saying!

'Your appearance definitely comes first, then your voice,' says voice and drama teacher John Noble, who also works as an actor, director and producer. He advocates dressing cleanly and appropriately 'to join the tribe'. When working with a team of accountants, for example, John will wear a suit. With a group of writers, he is more comfortable—and finds he gets a better response—dressed in casual clothes. By adopting a similar dress style to those around him, John is accepted more easily and obtains better results in his work.

Whichever style you select, 'Your appearance must be neat, clean and tidy,' says Julie Matthews, who, in addition to running Andrew Matthews Productions, presents seminars on business etiquette and corporate grooming. 'It does not have to be an expensive look,' she adds. 'Style is not governed by budget. Knowing *what* to wear is just as important. People make up their mind about you before you even open your mouth.' A smart outfit can boost a shy personality and give the wearer added confidence. An untidy and unkempt appearance can project an image of sloppiness and disorganisation.

Presentation goes far beyond dress sense. It extends to your manner and bearing. 'A firm and confident handshake is very important, as is good eye contact,' says Julie. A self-assured gait and posture also project confidence. A pleasant voice is another image winner. 'Your voice can change the first impression someone has of you, for better or worse,' says John Noble.

Working from home, you don't have to dress up unless there are clients in sight. 'I'm sitting here in my bathers,' says media consultant John Myers as we chat on the phone on a warm summer's day. 'In what other job would I be able to do that?'

Jenny Church of Your Type Secretarial Services says, 'I have found I don't need as many outfits as I used to. I still dress well, in business apparel, and wear make-up, but I have saved money on clothes.'

Some of us are able to work in a professional manner when casually dressed but others find it harder. Dressing casually can also lead to encounters of the embarrassing kind. When interior designer Catherine Bugoss first started working from home, she acknowledges that she found it hard to discipline herself. 'I would not dress up properly and it would take me forever to get round to starting work. I would do the dishes, put a load of washing on or decide that the garden needed weeding. Then I got caught in my pyjamas—by a client at 10.30 a.m.—and I decided I had to change my ways! From then on, I started dressing in business suits—as if I was going out to the office.'

Margaret Seedsman, National Executive Director of Home-Based Business Australia, says, 'I know of a worker who dresses smartly each morning, leaves the house and then walks back home from the nearest bus stop. He needs to do that to get himself in the right frame of mind to start work.' Margaret says it's also important to show clients you feel good about yourself and your business. But don't unbutton completely: 'A publicist once mentioned, in the midst of our telephone conversation, that she was lying by the pool, gin and tonic in hand. I thought that was going a bit far!'

When I am not meeting with others, I admit I tend to dress on the casual side. Yet I find that often, on days when I look smarter, my entire attitude is different. I feel more focused and efficient. I find it difficult to project a professional image—even on the telephone—when I'm in shorts and a T-shirt. But everyone is different.

Rosemary Stanton and her husband Peter both work from their rural NSW home, she as a dietitian and nutritionist and he as a computer programmer for clients in England. 'Peter has had many career changes,' Rosemary explains. 'Instead of going up corporate ladders, he goes down them—and his level of happiness increases. He has gone from wearing a suit, when working in engineering, to dressing casually and riding a bicycle when he worked as a teacher. Now he works from home in shorts or jeans. He believes the fewer constraints placed upon you, the higher your level of happiness and satisfaction—though not necessarily your income!'

Decide on your own dress and work style, which can vary according to the situation.

Will you be admitting clients into the private part of your home or just into your home office? Make sure all areas they're likely to see are clean and tidy at all times. A messy and cluttered environment will not inspire confidence. Not having a separate entrance and area for your business can be a disadvantage here.

'Clients come in our front door, so the house always has to be kept reasonably neat,' says Melbourne desktop publisher Maggie Boday, who works at home with her accountant husband Frank. 'Once inside, they might want to use the bathroom, so we have to make sure there are no wet towels or drying undies in there. There is a real lack of privacy—if the children have a shower, they are embarrassed to walk through the house in their dressing-gowns. We would prefer to have an outside office with a separate toilet and washbasin.'

Frank has discovered other disadvantages. 'Once you have an office at home, clients regard any meeting more as a social visit. They will stay around sitting and chatting about everything under the sun. You have to get the message across that this is business.'

'It's difficult to get some people to leave, short of being rude,' adds Maggie. 'I have had to excuse myself, saying that I have another appointment in ten minutes. I once left a client in the front lounge while I went to get some files from the office and returned to find him wandering through the house. Another time, someone arrived at 8 p.m. on a Friday to drop off his tax return. He brought his wife and children with him, and while we were talking in the office, the children went downstairs, turned on the computer and started fiddling with it. They seemed to have no respect for the fact that this was our home.'

Set your limits at the outset and make them obvious. It is up to you to make it clear that an interaction is a business meeting and not a social event. Obviously a balance has to be kept. Yet it is possible to enjoy a friendly and polite interaction while remaining firm about your boundaries.

It's much easier if you're lucky enough to have your office set apart from the house, or at least the main living areas. Adelaide homoeopath Meredith Norman has a separate entrance for her work premises, which are at the back of the house. 'Clients enter through the back door. They walk into a small passageway—on the right is my consulting room and on the left is the bathroom. Sliding doors provide a separation from the rest of the house. When I finish work on Saturday, I close all doors and don't come back until Monday. I would recommend a separate entrance wherever possible, so that you are not sharing the house with clients or strangers.'

Adelaide building designer Elvio Ferrara has gone one better and built himself a separate self-contained office at the rear of the family home. He has 32 square metres of space downstairs, which amply houses his drawing boards and files, table and chairs for client meetings, and a fully-equipped kitchen complete with hotplates. A panel in the ceiling opens to reveal an ingeniously designed ladder which provides an entrance to the upper level. Elvio has an additional 16 square metres of space here, presently unused. A toilet, sink and shower are located on the side of the heritage-style brick building. Clients and neighbours alike are impressed by the structure, which also serves as a valuable advertising tool. 'I am told by many that my environment reflects my good design abilities,' says Elvio, 'and the work is flooding in.'

Elvio, who has been working from home since 1990, built his home office in three months in 1995. It cost $30,000, and he believes that, by using recycled materials, he saved himself $10,000. 'Had I rented office premises, it would have cost me at least $10,000 a year. This office will serve me for ten or twenty years,' Elvio reasons. 'And I have room to expand upstairs. The offfice has added to the value of the house. The children can play and have sleepovers upstairs, and my wife and I can even live in here when we're oldies!'

Elvio found he needed an entirely separate work space to keep out noise—his two sons are aged six and three—and for his professional identity. There are still interruptions from friends and children, but Elvio uses this to his advantage and has developed strategies for dealing with dallying visitors. 'I have a system for friends who may drop in to see me—I remain standing, and they won't sit down unless I do. Sometimes I don't mind having a coffee with friends but, if it bothers me, I will say, "I've got work to get on with, I have a deadline." I'll walk them outside or suggest they go into the house for a coffee with my wife, Vassi, as they are likely also to be friends of hers.'

As for clients, 'I have meetings in here and young Michael may run in and say hello. The clients meet your family and I think that's important. It breaks down the formality, breaks down barriers and softens the image a little bit.'

It is up to you as to how you create an appropriate *balance* between a friendly, comfortable atmosphere and a professional image. It is necessary to set clients at ease while also giving them faith in your abilities. You must, however, consider security for yourself and for your home office. This is discussed in Chapter 8.

Your manner

A friendly, polite and courteous manner can work wonders. An angry attitude, however well-justified, will only serve to antagonise. 'Humility plays a big part in business and in life,' says Julie Matthews. 'Be humble. Nobody likes a big shot. People need to dress well, speak well, make good eye contact and be sincere in what they do. That's what people look for—sincerity. Some people working from home have an inferiority complex about doing so. They don't need to do that.

'You have to be *proud* that you work from home. Ask some people where they work and they'll swallow and mumble, "I only work from home." They are a little ashamed.' The truth is, there is nothing to be ashamed of in this regard and, indeed, much to be proud of—your independence, your self-motivation and your self-reliance are all fine attributes and qualities.

Your approach

This lays the foundation of your entire business. If you are disorganised, sloppy, disinterested, impatient or distracted, it will reflect badly on you and your business. And remember, it is one thing to be casual and friendly, but quite another to be offhand or abrupt. Make time for your clients. Make each one feel as if he is your most important customer, neither rushing him nor letting him completely dominate your time. Discover for yourself what a difference this makes.

The customer is always right!

Can this simple adage ever be stressed enough?

Think of it this way. If you do a $100 signwriting job and the customer is not satisfied, however hard you argue your case—that your work is of good quality and exactly what was ordered—you will not win. You may well be correct, but if the customer is not satisfied, what will you gain by arguing? Suppose you make your point and the customer pays up. How does this help you if he leaves in a huff, vowing never to come to you again, and then tells all his friends to avoid you?

Instead of fighting to prove you are in the right, you can be assertive while still looking after the customer's interests. Why not say, 'I did the work to the best of my ability and to the specifications we discussed. Yet you are not happy. My aim is to please you. So what would you like me to do?' Ask the customer if he wants the job altered or re-done, or if he wants a reduction in price. Even if he doesn't pay for the sign, at least you still have a satisfied customer. After all, it's hardly worth gaining $100 if you are then bad-mouthed around town. If you rely on repeat business, it is especially important that the matter be resolved amicably. Look at the lost $100 as advertising costs.

Photographer Matt Turner makes customer satisfaction an integral part of his business. 'If someone is not happy with my work, for whatever reason, then I won't charge at all,' he says. He would rather lose the money than goodwill, and he makes this clear to clients at the outset. In four years of working for himself, he has only once had to forgo a payment.

Learn to concede gracefully. To do so is a strength and not a weakness.

One way to immediately boost the productivity of your business is to decide to work *with* people rather than *against* them. Set out to assist your clients rather than placing obstacles in their way. A home-based business friend of mine was going overseas to attend a conference. Short of time, she telephoned the local branch of her bank to ask if they could have $3,000 worth of traveller's cheques ready for her to sign and pick up later that day.

Although she had an account there and was known to the staff, the bank employee presented her with a long list of reasons why this was not possible, concluding with the statement that she might not turn up to collect the cheques.

'Of course I will turn up, I *need* them,' she protested, but in vain. The employee would not be swayed, so my friend took her business—and account—elsewhere.

If you put obstacles in the way of your customers, you will alienate them. This is especially important with repeat customers. It is far easier to keep an existing customer than find a new one.

While you cannot expect to get on well with all your clients, they should all be offered the same care and consideration. 'I aim to please everyone, including rude people—and I have met a few of those,' says home-based electrician Bob Flaherty. 'But in fifteen years of working for myself, I have only had two disagreements. Mind you, I've had a lot of strong discussions!

'I go out of my way to prove to myself that no one is beyond the reach of courtesy. Besides, if you can please your customer, it's good advertising. You are just being pig-headed if you walk out of the situation. This is your future, after all. The whole essence of your business is customer service.' Yes, indeed—it's the customer who pays your wages!

'Do good work,' says Bob, 'and you will get more from the same source. I did some work for my accountant and this led to work for three of his partners and ten or so staff members.'

If people have a need, you need to be able to respond.

To make his customer service as prompt and efficient as possible, Bob has an answering machine at home. He also has a mobile telephone with a silent number. His wife and business partner, Sue, takes the answering machine messages and he calls in regularly 'or she can call me if it is an emergency,' Bob explains. (He believes taking calls constantly on his mobile phone 'is an imposition on the customer I'm with'.) He also has two back-up electricians he can contact at short notice. 'They handle any emergencies if I am busy. It doesn't happen very often—only 5 per cent of service calls are real emergencies—but I am prepared for any situation.'

While I was writing this, two light globes in my kitchen blew early in the morning. When I tried to change them, the bulbs broke off in my hand, leaving their metal collars behind. I called Bob and left a message on his answering machine, expecting to hear back from him that evening or the next day. Twenty minutes later, there was a ring at the doorbell. It was Bob.

How was that for customer service?

Jenny Church, of Your Type Secretarial Services, believes that to provide a good service, you should 'do all your work cheerfully and be very patient with people. Offer advice without involving yourself in a situation for which you could be liable.' Jenny is happy to present document layout or structural options if asked, but naturally the final decision and the responsibility for it belong to the client. 'Be as helpful as you can,' she says. 'Above all, honour your deadlines. If you have made a promise, stick to it!'

Your charges

We discussed how to set costs in Chapter 4. The secret is to stick to them, whether you are dealing with strangers, friends or acquaintances. Resist the temptation to do favours for friends. When word gets out, *all* your friends and acquaintances will come to expect a discount. Then what will you do? If you find charging for your work is difficult to handle, ask yourself: Are you running a business or a charity organisation? If you are happy, and can survive, on a reduced income, then well and good. Otherwise, stick to your charges for one and all.

Julie Matthews takes on the negotiations on fees for her husband Andrew. 'I market Andrew Matthews as a product,' she says. 'It would not be professional for Andrew to talk about money or terms and conditions.'

Offering everyone the same good service at the same price can, in fact, enhance your image and your standing. People believe they get what they pay for. A low price is equated with corner-cutting service and a cheap, inferior product. When people pay more, they are more likely to value the product or service. On the other hand, the occasional trade-off can be mutually beneficial. One home-based worker had a graphic designer friend prepare his business stationery at a discount and, in exchange, provided the friend with computer services at cost.

Home-based electrician Bob Flaherty says, 'My prices are not cheap but they are competitive. I must be doing something right, as I have never been out of work. Far from it. In fact, I had to stop advertising in the local papers, as I could not handle the amount of work generated. I have found from experience that a cheap price does not always win the job. I know of businesses where guys have taken the guts out of the prices and gone out of business in six months.'

Reliability

You may have found a large market. You may be offering the exact services your clients desire. You may have the right prices and you may be capable of doing the work well. But if you are unreliable, business is unlikely to boom.

Once you have made a commitment to a client, honour that commitment. Home-based architect Wayne Ketchen always makes sure he sets deadlines for projects, even when his clients have not already done so. 'That deadline can help me with motivation, as I know I am answerable to these people,' he explains. Whether a deadline is for your own sake or the client's, this is a good habit to cultivate. An additional tip is to try and *beat* your client's deadline. That way, you have a bit of leeway but if you do finish ahead of schedule you impress your client and boost your own confidence.

Jenny Church of Your Type Secretarial Services manages to meet constant deadline demands. 'The nature of my work is that I will have six people coming in daily, wanting the work completed yesterday. I cope, I've always lived like that. For me, business comes first, often before food and before family. I have been trained that way. I enjoy achieving challenges, doing the impossible, and I'm always thinking "how can I do it better?"' Jenny prides herself on her reliability and consequently her business is thriving.

Stick to your deadlines, and don't let your customers down.

That little bit extra

Naturally the quality of your work must be up to scratch. A professional manner or approach is unwarranted if your service or product lets you down. But what may not be quite so obvious is the benefit of providing that little bit extra—that additional service, that unexpected considerate touch. This will not only make you stand out from your competitors but demonstrate to the clients that you really do care about their patronage.

'After each project, we go back to the clients and ask whether they are happy with the service—whether we can help in any way, whether there is any problem we can fix,' says interior designer Catherine Bugoss. 'This has met with a great response. Clients are sometimes very surprised, and this can lead to other jobs. That little bit extra gets you noticed and remembered. It gets you more business, keeps the client happy and gives you self-satisfaction. If you leave a happy client and people later ask who did the work, he or she will happily pass on your details. Word of mouth is the best form of advertising.'

Window cleaner Josh Zappone, who works from his Adelaide home, also believes that 'little things count'. A new customer told him she had seen his ad in the local newspaper, offering 'a new generation of service'. 'She asked me what on earth could be new about window cleaning. I could see her point, but it's the little things that count.' Josh makes sure he brushes and cleans a window ledge before washing the window 'so that when you put water on it, it does not turn into a muddy mess'. He always places a towel underneath his bucket when working inside, so as not to drip water on the carpet. He cleans the flyscreens and removes cobwebs. 'Once you get rid of obvious cobwebs, the house really picks up. It has more impact and the whole thing looks really good. Clients appreciate that.'

They also appreciate the T-shirts that Josh and his wife, Emma, wear, emblazoned with their logo. 'When we go to someone's house, we don't just look like any other backyard person. The customer can see who we are straightaway,' says Josh. 'They can identify us and see we are a professional service. All our customers say, "Wow—that looks great. You look more professional each time we see you." And we've had many calls since we started wearing the T-shirts.'

What can *you* do in your business to elicit that 'wow' factor?

'When people book us for a seminar, we go just that little bit further than expected,' says Julie Matthews. 'We will help with their promotional flyers, designing them free of charge. We will do whatever we can to make their job a little easier.'

Don't keep the customer waiting

'People are getting used to answering machines,' says Marilyn Jolly of Jolly Home and Pet Care Service. 'I make a point of getting back to them as soon as possible, so that they feel they are not forgotten. I can take my messages from any location, simply by dialling a special access code.'

Window cleaner Josh Zappone also believes in responding swiftly to the needs of customers. 'When I was working for a subcontractor four days a week and for myself on the other day, customers would have to wait for me to attend to their needs. Now that I have my own business, I can do the work straightaway and customers like that,' he says. Even when Josh is very busy, he does not let his customers down. 'At those times my dad, who is also a window cleaner, shares the workload.'

REVIEW

A professional image is vital for business success. Never forget that *you* are the business.

You convey your image via:

- your *telephone manner*. Always identify yourself with your business name. Speak clearly, brightly and confidently. Be polite and helpful at all times. Regularly record a new message for your answering machine. Keep it brief, serious and to the point.
- the way you use *written or printed material*, such as stationery, promotional brochures and business cards.
- *face-to-face contact* with clients. This includes customer service. **Remember**, the customer is always right. A dissatisfied client will tell seventeen others, while a satisfied customer only tells three or four.

When dealing with your clients, create an appropriate *balance* between a friendly, comfortable atmosphere and a professional image. Offer each and every customer the same care and consideration. Be as helpful as you can. If people have a need, you need to be able to respond. Do all your work cheerfully and be patient with people. Honour your deadlines. Keep meetings friendly but business-like. Where possible, have a separate entrance to and area for your home office. Aim to give that little bit extra.

Respond promptly to your clients' needs.

ARTISTIC PURSUITS

Beate Wickert found a market and created a new industry in the process of working from home. Trained as a porcelain painter in Germany, her country of origin, she came to Australia with her architect husband, Jurgen, in 1986. 'There is no such industry here,' she explains. 'In Germany, there are two big manufacturers, who re-create the designs of the 1700s—that's how far back it goes. I worked for one of these manufacturers in Berlin and I would travel one-and-a-half hours each way to get to and from work. I used to leave home at 5.30 a.m. and I'd be completely exhausted by the time I arrived back home. I had hardly any private life. I would pass out in front of the TV. Now I can watch it while I work!'

When Beate and Jurgen came to Sydney, she started working from their accommodation, a large warehouse in Redfern. 'I found an agent in Sydney and another in Melbourne, and I'd give them samples of my work. I also started supplying trade fairs and goods by mail order.'

Beate paints beautifully detailed and intricate floral designs on to brooches and earrings, bracelets and little boxes, even on to business-card holders. She may have created a new enterprise but she had to compromise in the process. 'A brooch will cost $500 in Germany. Here you have to charge less than $20.'

The couple moved to Queensland in 1993, seeking a warmer climate and a more tranquil and outdoorsy lifestyle. 'I thought things would be difficult for me as I don't supply the shops in Cairns, it is not really the product for here,' Beate says. 'But it has turned out OK. I do business over the phone and fly to Sydney twice a year. I was worried that I would not be able to work from here, but my sales have doubled since last year.'

She works in an idyllic setting, a large room set aside especially for her work which has stunning views of lush tropical greenery. She overcomes any distractions by setting deadlines. Customer orders have to be completed in four to six weeks.

Making a living as a porcelain painter and also a jewellery manufacturer, Beate has shown the value of finding a new market as well as demonstrating that you can work from home anywhere.

The experience of Jennifer Woodhouse in Darwin shows just how adaptable a home-based career can be. A display artist by profession, Jennifer does window-dressing, arranges shop interiors and designs presentations at shows or exhibitions. Since 1986, she has been alternating between part-time and full-time home-based employment. 'I started off being home-based because of the very nature of the job,' Jennifer explains. 'I was freelancing rather than working for a particular company. That necessitated having a studio, so I converted a spare room at home into a studio rather than renting one, which would have been prohibitively expensive.'

When the demand for display work drops, Jennifer supplements her income by taking on other, outside work. She has worked as a receptionist in a chiropractor's office and as a sales assistant at weekends, over Christmas and during other busy times. 'I was able to work in the stores for which I did displays,' says Jennifer. So home-based work provided her with a connection that led to other jobs.

Working outside the home also helps overcome the problem of social isolation. 'I do find I miss that contact when I've worked at home for several days, as I'm a pretty gregarious person. But I will go out and meet with friends.'

'Discipline can be a difficulty when working from home. But I see it as more of an attitude adjustment. My work does not just involve one task such as sitting at a typewriter. I need to do lots of research and planning. I paint, make up objects . . . There are lots of possible angles, so if I get stuck on one, I can just move to another. I'm no good in a system. I don't like working in an organisation with people telling you what you can and can't do. My environment is very creative and I have the freedom to do what I want. I enjoy that sense of control, that ability to work late into the night or start early in the morning. When things get too much, when I get tired or the creative flow ebbs, then I'll do something basic like housework or shopping. I might garden. You can't stop and do that in an office.'

Another plus is that she doesn't have to make a full-time income. 'I'm lucky in that I do not have to support myself now. So that pressure is not there. I support my business, pay for my car and food, but my partner takes care of the other living expenses. Dean is very supportive. Not only does he show an interest in what I am doing but sometimes he also joins in.'

FOOD FOR THOUGHT

Shirley and Jeff Woods live in the shire of Corrigin, 250 km east of Perth. They have two 3,000-acre wheat and sheep farms. Dams on these farms contain yabbies. One of Shirley's children spotted a business opportunity here and suggested selling live yabbies to Perth. She applied for a licence from the Fisheries Department and started catching the yabbies in traps. Six years on, Shirley still supplies orders of up to 200 kg a week, catering for hotels and restaurants and selling wholesale to an exporter.

Some yabbies only had one claw because they'd fought over food. These were classified as seconds and fetched a lower price. 'Why should this be?' asked Shirley. 'Once cleaned, they are no different to the two-clawed ones. There is nothing wrong with them except their visual appearance.' She hit upon an idea and, like Beate Wickert the porcelain painter, created an entirely new enterprise. 'You can pickle gherkins and onions in jars, so why not yabbies?' Today you can purchase a jar of Kyalla Yabbies, savoury yabby tails resembling rounded jellybeans, at Myers in Perth and other major stores in WA.

Shirley had to overcome many obstacles in order to succeed. What began as a home-based occupation had to be relocated. 'I have to work in a little hall at Bullaring, ten minutes' drive away. The law did not allow me to work from home unless I had certain things in place such as a concrete floor, special lighting, taps that could be turned on with your foot. "Why do I need a concrete floor?" I asked. I am not filleting fish, I'm not an abbatoir. But no one had ever done what I was intending to do and they did not know how to handle it.' Minor renovations had to be done at the hall in order for it to comply with Health Department regulations.

Shirley employs local women to work with her one day a week. 'It's a bit like a chain reaction,' she explains—each person dealing with a different job until the cooked and peeled yabby tails end up in sealed jars. Shirley makes 20 kg of savoury yabbies a week as well as fulfilling her live yabby orders from home. Interest has built up since she first exhibited the product at Perth's Food-Fest in 1994.

She can see good potential in it. 'This could be another great export industry for Australia, like wheat and wool. There are yabbies throughout the country and we already export over 300 tons of live yabbies annually.'

Shirley has learnt much about yabbies, and the food industry, and been somewhat discouraged. 'The yabbies have to be purged before cooking. Removing any mud or sediment gives them a better and sweeter taste. The ingredients are listed on the jar, in order from the largest to the smallest. A date is put on as well as the place they were made. My yabbies are the only ones in Australia that have a six-month shelf life. No refrigeration is necessary. I pay over $600 a year for a fish farm licence for the live yabbies and a process licence for the savoury ones. The food hygiene reading on my savoury yabbies—which looks at micro-organisms in the food—is far better than state requirements. Yet I am not allowed to export as the regulations are so strict. For export I would require an anteroom for people to have their tea, different windows in the building, and so on. I almost gave up along the way. It was as if the goose that laid the golden egg was being cooked!'

Market gardeners Frank and Annie Ackland-Prpic have found their business is an ever-growing one. When they started growing herbs at the end of 1982, the market was not yet established. They had purchased a property at Victor Harbor, South Australia, with the intention of growing vegetables. But this proved to be too fiddly and only a seasonal occupation. When their seed merchant told them that agents were buying chive seeds to grow for their customers, as fresh chives were not available, the Ackland-Prpics increased their mixed-herb numbers. A friend offered to sell basil and chives for them in his fruit and vegetable store and the couple became one of the first in the herb and salad industry.

Another boost to their business came when the herb farm at Yatala Jail was closed down after a change in the state government. They met with the gardener, who not only gave them plants and cuttings, but also offered helpful advice on growing herbs, supplementing their knowledge.

Today Annie and Frank live with their daughters on a property at Montacute, twenty minutes' drive from the centre of Adelaide. They grow 25 herbs—including thyme, sage and coriander—a selection of salad greens, lemons and some cherries. Work can be a social and family occasion, with friends and relations helping with picking and packing and the children designing labels for 'A-Pic' herbs. 'The children realise what is involved in making a living,' Annie says, 'but the downside is working evening after evening at busy times. You would not commit yourself to daily overtime in an outside job.' Working for yourself, there are no sick days either. 'The job has to be done whether you're feeling ill or not,' says Frank. 'You can't take a sickie.' 'We work seven days a week,' says Annie, 'with Frank doing most of the seeding, the ploughing and tractor work while I concentrate on the bookwork and help with the picking and the packing. I can spend the weekend with the children but it is harder for Frank. He is always at his job, but then again, the children do see him. I think working with your partner can enrich your relationship. You learn to listen to one another more, to value the other's judgments. Each person has different abilities. Frank is doing the growing while I see things from the customer's side. We used to cut the coriander at ground level and bunch it, but now that Thai cooking is so popular, we sell the whole plant, roots and all.'

Frank and Annie sell to the wholesale market through agents. 'When we started, this was all new,' says Annie. 'Rocket (arugula) was fairly unknown. Now it is a big seller, as are the other herbs. There are a lot more growers now but the market is much larger. So it's all right.'

Edgar Wakefield has fond recollections of his childhood in South Africa, living in the country town of George, an agricultural centre. 'It was an idyllic lifestyle and those memories have never left me,' he says. After arriving in South Australia twenty years ago, at the age of 33, he spent many years working as a teacher before taking a redundancy package in 1993. 'Teaching has changed, it has become very stressful,' he explains. 'It is no longer student- or people-centred. The rights of students and teachers are not being addressed, and I was very unhappy.'

He decided to change his lifestyle completely and start a business growing mixed vegetables. Recently remarried, he was contemplating buying a shop. But after looking at his first year's earnings, he realised this was not a viable proposition. Edgar was growing his produce in the garden of his wife Beverley's property at Murray Bridge, an hour's drive from Adelaide. 'There were lots of native trees there, mature gums and eucalyptus. I could see possibilities. We designed and built a mud-brick house in which we now live.'

Meanwhile Beverley, who had been working for Telstra in middle management, developed arthritis in the knees and took a redundancy package in 1994. 'We share a love for nature, we're both conservationists,' says Edgar. 'Beverley is a marvellous gardener, while I did not know a great deal. We had a pilot planting on the property to see what would grow there and started with cauliflower, broccoli, corn and pumpkin. We tried compost and natural fertiliser and applied for certification as organic gardeners with NAASA, the National Australian Association of Sustainable Agriculture. They test your soil for pesticides and herbicides and ensure you are using sound organic practices. This certification gives us the ability to sell interstate.'

Edgar now grows zucchinis and has established a market for his home-grown gem squash, which happens to be a large export-earner for South Africa. 'I walked the streets of Adelaide to crack the market,' he says. 'I built up business by word of mouth, going to the shops and speaking to the owners. That took me fifteen months. South Australia can be quite conservative. People are suspicious of something new on the market and you have to convince them. I would give gem squash, free of charge, to stores and include cooking instructions and recipes.'

Riverglades naturally-grown products have proved popular and Edgar appreciates being his own boss. 'I make the decisions and negotiate the prices. I like the person-to-person contact in shops.' He has planted many native plants on the Murray Bridge property and done a lot of landscaping. The mud-brick house in which he and Beverley live blends into the surrounds and is cool in summer and warm in the winter. It is a quiet lifestyle. 'The flowers bloom summer and winter. It is very peaceful and beautiful here. I enjoy that at this time of my life,' says Edgar, who has managed to recapture those idyllic times of his childhood.

6

SELLING YOURSELF AND YOUR BUSINESS

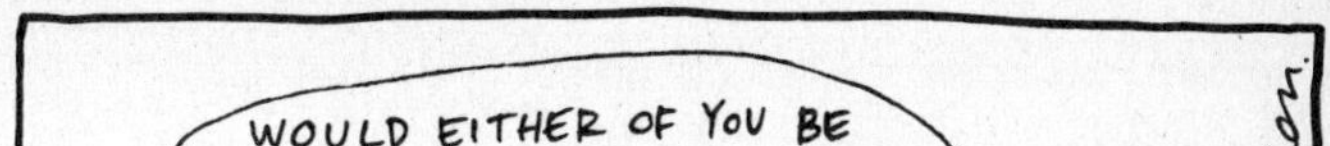

The initial hard work has been done. Your business is up and running. You are satisfied that your service and products are of high quality and that there is a market for them. You have done your research well, checking out your competitors and pricing accordingly. You've thought of everything. Or have you?

How are people to know of your new business and the goods and services that you offer? They may be the best, but if no one has heard of you, then all your efforts have been wasted. It is time to think about marketing!

Making yourself known

'Some are born great, some achieve greatness and others use public relations.' There is much truth in this humorous caption I saw prominently posted on a friend's noticeboard. Public relations influences the way customers see your business. The *Macquarie Dictionary* defines public relations as 'the practice of promoting goodwill among the public for a company' and 'the practice of working to present a favourable image'.

Public relations encompasses *advertising*, *promotion* and *publicity*. Depending on your circumstances and your budget, you can organise these elements yourself or else hire someone else to do so for you. Names of accredited individuals or organisations may be obtained from your state branch of the Public Relations Institute of Australia.

With *advertising*, because you are paying you have total control. If you advertise in a newspaper or magazine, you can select the size and position of your ad and the frequency of its appearance. You can make radio or television commercials. You can buy billboard spaces and fill them with posters advertising your product or service.

Promotions or special offers can encourage people to use your products or services. A 10 per cent discount for any typing job of more than 50 pages is an example of a promotion in action. Promotions can be used to generate business at quiet times. One picture framer offers 25 per cent off for any work done in January, to boost a low business period when many of her customers are away on holiday.

Publicity can be detrimental as well as beneficial to your business. Some would argue that there is no such thing as bad publicity—after all, it makes your product and business known to the public. But, if a newspaper food writer notes that your jams are bitter and unpleasant-tasting, customers will hardly be queuing up to buy!

Should you advertise?

Think about the brand of toothpaste you use, the breakfast cereal you eat, the kind of car you drive. Can you recall the slogans or ads used to promote them? You may *imagine* you are a free-thinking person who is not influenced, let alone manipulated, by advertising, but if you really think about what has made you select certain products and not even consider others, you may well be surprised.

Although advertising can indeed be effective, you still need to ask yourself whether you need it. Perhaps your business will build up purely through word-of-mouth recommendations.

This is the most effective way for a small business to become known. And it's free.

If someone you trust recommends an accountant to you—one who is pleasant, reliable and has got your friend a $3,000 tax rebate last year—you are far more likely to try that accountant than to choose one at random from the *Yellow Pages*.

Photographer Matt Turner has not spent a cent on advertising. His work has all come to him by recommendation—from journalists he knows, from other photographers with too much work on, from satisfied customers. This is not only good for Matt but means his clients come to him with faith in his abilities.

'When I needed some business cards made up, my friend Susan told me of a home-based graphic designer. I was so impressed with his services that I told another friend who in turn spread the word among colleagues at her legal practice. I worked out that that one recommendation from Susan to me had led to five other recommendations. How many other people had Susan told?'

But active promotion is important, too. At a talk given at Adelaide's Marketing Week a few years ago, I noticed round yellow stickers attached to the backs of chairs and pillars. Attracted by their bright colour, I looked more closely and read the words, 'Never miss an opportunity to market yourself'. It was a brilliant and effective advertising concept—and also a maxim well worth adhering to.

You may think you have invented the most environmentally sound cat litter ever. Recycling old newspapers was such a splendid idea! But if nobody knows about your amazing new product, you're stuck with ten tonnes of newsprint. The windows you clean may sparkle brightly because of your technique and the cleaning fluid you have designed. But if no one knows where to contact you, you'll be spending your days alone at home—with a clear but unpromising outlook.

Assess the market

If you want to follow this excellent advice, the first thing you need to do is consider your market—the customers you want to reach.

If you have prepared a business plan, you will already have identified your market and compiled a customer profile. Review this and consider:

- the spread of your market. Does it cover your suburb, the entire state, the country? Does it extend overseas?
- the age of your customers
- their special needs or interests
- whether your customers are individuals or companies

The answers will help you work out the best way to approach publicity. They will also save you money. It is surprising how many companies waste big dollars by advertising in inappropriate areas. If you are manufacturing or selling personal alarms for the elderly, for example, it would be appropriate to send information to local retirement villages. If you are making wetsuits, it makes sense to advertise in scuba-diving magazines and sports stores.

On the other hand, it would be costly, ludicrous and ultimately unprofitable to advertise on national television when you are a small, locally-based company that can only supply goods and services in a 20 km radius. And advertising in a pop music magazine is unlikely to elicit much response for your lessons in opera singing.

Low-cost publicity

Publicity isn't necessarily expensive. There are many ways to promote your business at low—or no—cost.

You could do a letterbox drop of potential customers in your area. Marilyn Jolly distributes leaflets for her home and pet care business at local veterinary surgeries and pet shops. One satisfied client recommended her services to her vet, which resulted in considerable new business for Marilyn.

You can distribute your card and brochures at any business meetings you attend. Or at any other opportunity. A van ahead of me at the traffic lights one day bore the sign 'Caution—blind man driving'. Intrigued, I accelerated to overtake once the lights changed and caught sight of the confident-looking driver, who was wearing dark glasses. I was flummoxed. It took me some time to realise that this 'blind man', far from being visually impaired, made up and installed window blinds! I later spoke with him and he told me how on one occasion he had leapt out of his van at the traffic lights, wearing his sunglasses, pretended to stumble to the car alongside and thrust his business card through the open window at the amazed occupants. Who will *they* think of the next time they need blinds?

Design some flyers to be slipped into magazines in waiting rooms. One home worker provides arrangements of her dried flowers for free at the local dental surgery—on condition that it display her business card.

Use your answering machine. Dial Marilyn Jolly's number and, if she is unavailable, you will hear the following message:

> Hi, this is Jolly Home and Pet Care. We can't get to the phone right now but here are some of the services we provide while looking after your pets in your house. We walk dogs, clear letterboxes and papers, feed and water all pets, water pot plants, put out the rubbish bin and check the house daily. Our prices are from $12 a visit. If you'd like more information, please leave your name and number after the beep and we will get back to you.

Marilyn made up this message out of consideration for potential customers. 'We found most of the people who call us want general facts,' she explains, 'so we put in the information they were most likely to ask for. It works really well—they feel they have not wasted a telephone call, and we are not spending time going over the same information. It saves telephone calls on both sides. Now when people ring, we know it is most likely to be a genuine inquiry for our services.'

One home-based business has magnetic car signs, which can be removed easily at times when the owners don't wish to be identified. You may not want to be known as Larry's Landscaping Services when you attend a friend's barbecue—though for a small-business owner, such occasions are few and far between! Bear in mind that maintaining a professional image is critical when you have a logo on your vehicle. Screeching around corners and exceeding the speed limit are not a good move for Larry's Landscaping Services nor for Larry's bank balance.

Window cleaner Josh Zappone has had T-shirts emblazoned with his business logo. Whenever he and his wife Emma are working, they are broadcasting their services to other potential clients.

Approach potential customers in person. Catherine Bugoss scours newspapers and magazines for stories on the latest building projects. She then approaches the companies with her interior design portfolio, and this has resulted in big work contracts. One home-based food company approached a major airline with its gourmet jams and found an untapped, and large, market. A children's writer approached libraries and obtained regular speaking engagements. While most of these were unpaid, they helped increase her profile, which resulted in larger sales of her books, and also enabled her to 'test-run' new stories on her ready-made audience.

Cross promotion is another cost-effective idea. You can combine with another home-based business to offer the public a more complete service package. As a photographer, you can team up with a graphic designer. As a house-cleaning service, you can recommend a lawnmowing business, and vice versa. Teaming up can help mutual promotion and cut advertising costs.

You can advertise inexpensively in home-based business newsletters and publications. I have found that home-based businesses tend to support one another and endorse each other to potential clients, which is terrific. Who better to promote you and your home-based business than someone in a similar situation? Before you know it, you can build up a network of home-based businesses that you can recommend and ones that will, in return, recommend you and your business.

Don't neglect regular customers either. By giving them special service you can encourage them to promote your business for you. Marilyn Jolly gives her regular clients slightly cheaper rates if they introduce her to new clients. That's an innovative and efficient way of building up business.

Finally, you can use the media inexpensively. Put together a newsworthy story about your business and send it as a media release to the local newspaper, radio and television stations. Or send a funny anecdote about your business to the newspaper. This may be used as a short filler, your business name appearing as a by-product, and hopefully a buy-product!

Advertising

Suppose you've decided you could use paid advertising. The first thing to consider is:

Are you allowed to advertise?

For most occupations, the answer is yes. But in certain professions there are strict rules governing advertising. When I worked as a dentist in private practice in the Northern Territory in 1980, I was permitted to place a small notice in the local newspaper stating that I had commenced work at the practice. This notice was allowed to be published weekly, three times in all. Any further advertising would not have been acceptable to the local Dental Board. Doctors' advertising is also restricted. As a lawyer or an accountant, you *can* advertise. If you specialise in family law, for example, or in tax returns, you can state this and seek clients accordingly.

Can you afford to advertise?

If you decide that paid advertising is necessary for your home business, set aside part of your budget, and your time, for it. That budget does not have to be vast. Advertising whiz Simon Reynolds—best-known for the Grim Reaper television commercial—suggests 2 per cent of sales for big business and 5 per cent of sales for small business.

But you should be careful *how* you spend the money. It is possible to waste thousands of dollars with no impact on your sales. Ask yourself if your ad spending is likely to have a profitable result. Speak with others in the same line of business. Ask the publication or organisation with whom you intend advertising about the best line of action. It may be far more effective to advertise in the newspaper each Saturday, when there are more readers, than on several weekdays. Late-night television commercials may be more likely to reach your target audience than daytime ones.

At this stage, you may choose to hire a public relations person or firm to advise on and organise a public relations campaign. Again, this will be geared to your budget and your needs. You may need to advertise only initially, gradually winding down the campaign as your business becomes established and repeat customers are found. Be prepared to pay a public relations person at least $80 an hour. The alternative is to negotiate a total package for a fixed amount.

Where to advertise

When considering the media, there are *print* and *electronic* media. *Print* outlets include local, national, suburban and rural newspapers, magazines, trade journals and professional publications, mailing lists, club and society newsletters, home-based business association booklets, and the *Yellow Pages* telephone directory. It may be appropriate for you to advertise or insert a profile piece in newletters, trade journals or professional publications. This is known as advertorial, as opposed to editorial, content. You pay for advertorial, which resembles an article rather than an advertisement. The words 'advertisement' or 'advertising material' must appear at some spot on an advertorial page.

The electronic media comprise radio and television.

Print

When purchasing advertising space in a print outlet:

- choose an appropriate publication which your potential customers are likely to read
- have an eye-catching advertisement designed by a professional
- make sure your ad is a good size, and well-positioned, such as in the top right-hand corner, near the front of the newspaper
- make sure your ad is run long enough and regularly enough to make an impact

When looking at paid advertising, you can also consider radio and television outlets. This may not be as expensive as you think. By selecting appropriate timeslots, you can get good value for money and worthwhile results for your business.

The rates for late-night and early morning advertising on television are economically priced and, if your potential client falls into this target audience, you may like to think of using some of your advertising budget here. Likewise, radio can offer good deals for a series of ads in your campaign. Check with your local radio and television stations for further details.

Evaluation

The difficulty with advertising and promotion is that no one can guarantee results. What may have worked for a business colleague may not, for a variety of reasons, work for you. You can experiment, having a trial run with a few advertisements, and gauging the reaction. *Ask each new client how they came to hear of you and your business. Take good note of the answers.* Was it through an advertisement or by way of an individual who was pleased with your work? Did they see the logo on your car or spot your snazzy T-shirt? Was your letterbox drop successful or did your leaflets, prominently displayed in a local shop, do the trick?

Don't expect too high a response rate to your ad. Have you ever returned to your car after a night out and found a leaflet on the windscreen? Perhaps it boasts that it can give you the secret of losing weight easily and quickly or invites you to a local nightclub at a discount upon presentation of the leaflet. If *you* patiently placed such leaflets on 1,000 car windscreens, how many responses do you think you would get? If you got just 20 positive replies, you would be doing well! The same applies to mail-outs. Post out 100 leaflets and if you get two or three sales, you'll be pleased. Telephone salespeople are considered highly skilled if they make one sale in every ten calls.

But do not let this news disillusion you. Be aware. Be sensible about the ways in which you can market your business.

Retain a healthy scepticism about the benefits of paid advertising. Learn more about how it operates and look at the ways in which it can operate most economically and most effectively for you.

The media release

You can get what amounts to free advertising if you are able to get a story about your business run in the newspaper or on radio or TV. You do this with a media release, a short, preferably one-page, summary of a prospective story that can be used for an article, feature, news item or interview. The idea is that once people read the article, see the show or hear you speak on radio or television, they will know about your business and hopefully buy your goods or use your services.

So *how* do you put together a media release? Let us suppose you have started a home-based business providing graphic design services. Many graphic designers work from home. What is different, what is unusual, what is *newsworthy* about your business? 'News' is 'new information, fresh events'. News can be about the first or the last, the biggest or the smallest. News is something different, something out of the ordinary, something unusual. Say you have recently secured a lucrative contract with a hotel chain in Singapore—and you're the first Australian graphic design firm to do so. Now, *that* is news.

You may paint porcelain brooches with Australian scenes, which you sell to souvenir stores in Sydney, Perth and Melbourne. You discover that most of your customers are overseas tourists, many of them German. They are delighted to take a 'little piece of Australia' home with them. The funny thing is, you yourself are from Germany. Not only are you now promoting your adopted country, but you have also introduced a new skill to that country. Porcelain painting is a traditional and highly-respected profession in Germany, but relatively unknown here. This too is newsworthy, and articles and interviews can be constructed around it. These sorts of things are the 'angles' for which journalists are always looking.

That's all well and good, you may say, but I run a home-based typing service—or an electrical business—and there is nothing new or different about me. Or is there? The fact that you are a *man* running the typing service is unusual in itself. By now you may be used to the response of surprised customers who expect to see a woman. Their reactions might make an interesting newspaper story. As an electrician, you may have two customers who avoided serious house fires thanks to the smoke detectors you installed. This might be a good introduction to a story in which you discuss the importance of these potentially lifesaving devices.

Are you starting to get the hang of it?

A media release should answer the following questions: Who, what, why, when, where, how? Cover all those points and you will have covered your story! You can put together and send out the media release yourself or hire a public relations person or company to do this for you.

Let us look at an example.

MEDIA RELEASE

For the attention of Susan Jeffries, News Editor, *The Daily Times*
7 November 1997
Embargoed until 8 November 1997

Local business wins big overseas contract

Twenty-year-old Meredith Summers has become the youngest Australian small-business owner to ever win a large overseas contract. Her home-based business has secured a lucrative contract, worth $500,000 over five years, for translation services, with a Japanese firm.

Language Links, which has been operating for just twelve months, impressed the Tokyo company with its high-quality, reliable and speedy service. Meredith, who uses the latest computer equipment, has been able to secure the work despite stiff competition. Having visited Japan several times, she has proved that distance is no object when it comes to finding business.

'I'm absolutely thrilled to have won the contract,' says Meredith. 'I have found that being home-based is an advantage. To me, the secrets of success are marketing yourself well, being confident in your ability and being totally dedicated.'

For further information, please contact Meredith Summers on tel 042 123 4567, fax 042 123 4555, mobile 041 123 456. She is available for interview.
Black-and-white photograph or colour transparency provided on request.

Where to send it

Your media release can be posted or faxed to newspaper and magazine, radio and television journalists. In considering where to send it, ask yourself: What is your market? Is this a local story or will it have national interest? State and many local libraries will have a copy of *Margaret Gee's Australian Media Guide*, which lists details of newspapers and magazines throughout the country. This is a good starting point.

When considering local and national newspapers, do not forget suburban or rural ones. You may, in fact, have more success with them. Remember also community newspapers and newsletters, ethnic newspapers and magazines, and specialist publications. There is a large magazine market, including trade journals and professional publications which may also be suitable.

The electronic media, too, have a voracious and relentless appetite for stories. While newspapers have fixed space in each edition for these stories, radio and TV news bulletins change throughout the day, so particularly on local radio you have more chance of getting a story in. You also have a better chance of securing an interview on radio talk and current affairs shows or special-interest shows. Local morning TV shows can also be good to target.

Address the media release to the appropriate individual at the company—the news editor or the business journalist on a paper, the producer or presenter of the radio or television show you are approaching. Do make sure you know the program well and that your story is appropriate. Sending a media release about your tulip exporting business to a local TV cookery show is hardly likely to result in an interview!

If aiming at television news or current affairs, think of the *visual* angle. Shots of your colourful tulips would suit.

Timing

When is it appropriate to send out your media release? This depends on a few factors. Is your story relevant only for a short time? How often does the publication you are targeting come out? If it is a daily newspaper, one or two days' notice will be sufficient. If it is a weekly newspaper, give one to two weeks' notice.

Timing is all-important. Give too much notice of the event or occurrence and your media release may be put aside and forgotten. Give too little notice and it may be too late for the journalist to organise a story.

When faxing, first thing in the morning is the best time.

Getting your release noticed

How can you maximise the chances that your media release will be singled out from the many hundreds of others and acted upon?

Make sure:

- It is unusual and newsworthy.
- It is addressed to, and reaches, the right person at the right time. Never send information addressed to just a radio or TV station. For which program and for which person is it intended?
- It is clear. Make your story short, snappy and direct. Give as much information as you can in the fewest words. Use straightforward English.
- It is professionally and appealingly presented. You might use colour or bold graphics to make it stand out.
- It is followed up with a polite telephone call, asking whether any further details are required.
- You are readily available for interviews.

Journalists are always working to deadlines. Their time is short and the easier you can make things for them, the happier they will be and the more likely it is that your story will be picked up.

Your media release may be quoted word for word in a newspaper article. Be prepared for this. Then congratulate yourself that you pitched its style and content correctly!

The interview

The best way to handle an interview is: *prepare, prepare, prepare.* Prepare what you want to say and how you will say it. Ask the person who is organising the interview a few key questions—how long is the interview likely to last, what will be its focus, and—if for radio or television—will it be live or pre-recorded?

Prepare how you will look. Dress smartly and appropriately. Arrive punctually. Have supporting material on hand—a copy of your media release, and a photograph or transparency for a newspaper or magazine. Note your main points and jot these down on a piece of paper. You can refer to them before or during your interview to calm your nerves. Be friendly and helpful, courteous and charming.

Handle butterflies by concentrating on *enjoying* what you are doing. This is, after all, an opportunity for you to talk about the business you have established. You are talking about a subject in which *you* are the expert, about which *you* know more than your interviewer. And you might even inspire others. You only have to look at the number of biographies and autobiographies in print to know that what people are most interested in is other people and their lives.

Once you start the interview, you will most certainly find it a pleasurable experience. A radio interview will be much more memorable and impressive if you create word pictures rather than reciting facts or discussing abstract concepts: 'Since I re-designed the packaging for my gourmet jams, I have saved ten trailer-loads of waste cardboard a year,' rather than '. . . I have saved two tons of waste cardboard a year.' Use anecdotes to make a point and use humour as much as possible. Keep your answers short and to the point. A radio interview may only last five minutes and if you take ages answering the first question, there won't be much time for more.

REVIEW

Public relations influences the way customers see your business. It encompasses advertising, publicity and promotion.

You pay for and have total control over *advertising*, deciding on the size and position of your advertisement and the frequency of its appearance.

Promotions can be used to sell your products or services.

Publicity can be free.

How to market your business

- Identify and target your market.
- Aim at repeat business, offering discounts or special offers to encourage this.
- Money-back guarantees can also buoy up business.

Building up your profile

You can consider:

- a letterbox drop of potential customers in your area;
- buying an advertisement in your local newspaper;
- preparing a media release for your local newspaper, radio and television stations; and
- sending a funny anecdote about your business to your local newspaper.

You must:

- maintain a professional image at all times; and
- always be aware of providing good personal service.

Advertising in action

- Contemplate print and electronic (radio and television) outlets.
- Consider cross-promotions.

For print advertising

- Choose an appropriate publication to attract potential clients.
- Have an attractive, eye-catching and appealing advertisement design.
- Choose an appropriate size and prominent position for your advertisement to be noticed.
- Ensure your advertisement is run long enough and regularly enough to make an impact.

Never miss an opportunity to market your business.

Your media release

A *media release* is a short summary of a story about your business, sent to a media outlet, and designed to encourage an article or interview.

Make sure your media release is:

- timed correctly;
- unusual and newsworthy;
- answers the questions—who, what, why, when, where and how?;
- is addressed to the right person in the right department;
- is no longer than one A4 typed page in length;
- uses clear and direct language;
- gets across the most information in the least number of words;
- has an appealing and professional presentation;
- is followed up with a polite telephone call, asking whether further details are required; and
- includes the details of a person readily available for interview.

How to handle an interview

Prepare, prepare, prepare.

Engaging in and enjoying the interview

- arrive on time and be well-presented
- have your main points written down and memorised
- adopt a confident manner
- speak slowly and clearly
- be personable, friendly and helpful
- answer all questions concisely and stick to the point
- be enthusiastic and smile
- show respect to the interviewer
- relax, and keep your sense of humour

Never miss an opportunity to market your business

Lying back in the dental chair, my mouth wide open and in a state of panic, I was distracted by a sign on the ceiling, 'If you are happy with your treatment, please tell your friends. If not, please keep your mouth shut.'

That dentist certainly took every chance of building up business!

Window cleaner Josh Zappone also has an innovative approach. 'I carry my business cards in my top pocket,' he says, 'and when I am working on some shop windows or a house, I aim to get more jobs in the same shopping centre or the same street.'

He will assess, for example, the store next door. Then, business card in hand, he walks in saying, 'Hi, I've just started my own business. If you ever want your windows cleaned, I can do it for $5.' He immediately identifies himself, gives a price and, not surprisingly, the work rolls in!

DRAWING A COMPARISON

Have you ever wondered who creates those artistic and detailed drawings of houses for the real estate pages of the newspaper? Chances are, it will be a home-based worker—someone like Rod Hutchison. Although a sole practitioner, he is one of a highly skilled group who do work for real estate companies. He describes himself as an illustrator, also doing technical drawings. These can range from sketches for an Air Force workshop manual to representations of airconditioning valves. But the bulk of his work is in real estate.

Rod is self-taught. 'I was a technician for the Air Force and, when I left, I was out of work for a month before finding a job in the Commonwealth public service,' says Rod. He spent that time sketching stone buildings. When a real estate agent happened to see his illustration of a stone smokehouse on the Nairne property Rod and his wife had purchased, he commented that it would look good in the newspaper.

'Nobody else was using this process of illustration back then, in 1972,' says Rod. 'The only line drawings in the newspaper were of project houses. So I started doing these real estate drawings on a part-time basis.'

In the meantime, he did other varied work, including in aged care. When a five-year contract ended in August 1990, he had built up sufficient work in illustration to enable him to work full time in his home-based business.

'I had several customers in the late 1980s and I was going quite well, earning a good $5,000 for illustrations in addition to my other income. I now have a fully-equipped studio at home and I'll be at my desk, in my pyjamas, at seven in the morning. I'll have breakfast an hour later and get on with my day.'

Rod's wife also works in the business—doing administration, answering the phone and sometimes delivering sketches. They are a partnership and have a registered business name, Hutchison Illustrators.

Rod built up his workload by advertising in Real Estate Institute magazines as well as approaching agents face to face. He has also taught himself to do floor plans and site plans. He has a set price for his work, which does not vary despite the size of a house or the travel involved for him. He will do pencil sketches of the house at the location, measure up the interior and complete the work at his home. 'What I lose on the swings, I gain on the roundabouts,' he says. 'That takes care of fluctuations.' As for separating work and free time, 'depending on the workload, I'll aim to finish by Friday afternoon so I'll have a slightly extended weekend,' says Rod.

Craig Smith has illustrated more than 140 books in his twenty-year career. Self-discipline has never been a problem for him. 'Small business is in the blood,' he says. 'My parents ran a shoe store in the Adelaide Hills and I put an enormous amount of stress on their example. They never demanded that I be my own boss but it seemed a perfectly natural thing to do. I have no fear of being self-employed. To me, it is almost genetic,' Craig smiles.

When he started work, it was from home. 'Traditionally a lot of book illustrators go to art school, then work from the bedroom and don't emerge until their mid-30s,' he laughs. 'And being shy seems to go with the work. Perhaps you take refuge from the real world in the finicky reworking of images and textures.'

Maybe. Yet Craig's work, like that of other illustrators, has brought delight to thousands of youngsters. His versatile style has seen him illustrate books as diverse as *The Giant's Tooth* by Gillian Rubinstein, *The Cabbage Patch Book* by Paul Jennings and *Billy the Punk* by Jessica Carroll. Several of the publications on which he has worked have won prestigious awards, and his clients include the likes of Australia Post as well as Australia's major book publishers.

But talent is not enough. One of the hardest aspects of Craig's work is forcing himself to overcome his shyness and get out of the house in order to establish work contacts. 'A normal working environment gives you incidental contacts. It is important to meet people, that is the stuff of work,' he believes. 'People say it is cheaper in overheads working from home. But artists do not realise that work flows in by word of mouth. One of the immediate advantages of working in a commercial studio is that you are in a business loop. The set-up almost pays for itself as you end up getting more work.'

It was only after Craig and his wife Lisa started a family that Craig left his home work base. 'It became an intolerable situation with a newborn baby, and our relationship suffered as a consequence. A friend offered me space in his graphic design studio, so I worked from there.'

For the next few years, Craig worked away from home and spent a few years in an Adelaide studio with other illustrators and designers. 'We all worked independently but there was a certain amount of crossover. We subcontracted amongst ourselves, which was good. As time went on, I found the buzz and innovative feedback ceased and staleness set in, along with dull routine. It was no longer exciting. After you have been with a group for so long, how do you revitalise it? And do you expect to be revitalised by other people anyway if you're basically individualistic?'

Craig was also worn out by meeting all the bills. 'It was my responsibility to pay them as they came in, then we would divvy it up. I was always aware of the work flow of others and sometimes I might not be repaid for a couple of months.'

As it happened, the studio was broken into, later suffered a couple of arson attacks and was eventually gutted. This left the occupants uneasy, and it seemed an appropriate time for Craig to leave the group and return to working from home. He is now very concerned with security and he is pleased to be at his premises all the time.

'At first it was surprising to go from a very gregarious environment to being alone again. You can feel lonely and isolated working from home if you don't know how to remedy it. The downside of working from home and so not interacting routinely with people is that you can lose the ability to string words or thoughts together. You lapse into a silent routine, as you are alone much of the time.'

Craig counteracts this with his involvement with schools. Book Week in August is a particularly busy time for him. He also makes sure his work is not at the expense of family time. 'I work five days a week and rarely past six in the evening. I work shorter hours than I did in the office. I've learnt to be more efficient, and when I have a deadline, I'll get up earlier.'

Home-based architect Wayne Ketchen has found being able to watch his two children grow up an invaluable experience. 'With flexible working hours, I can have plenty of contact with the family,' he says, 'but you do need to develop strategies.' For Wayne, that includes such approaches as playing with the children during the day and making up the work time later on, or allowing his young son to draw alongside him.

'I do find I now have a lack of contact with other professionals, so I will make an effort to drive out and see people. I attend seminars and certainly do not sit at home and vegetate. Clients can view you differently when you work from home. But it is certainly not true that if you are working from home you can't make it elsewhere. You do need to have a professional presentation, be reasonably smartly dressed and have the image associated with this. I have not found any loss of status in working from home. In fact I have developed more self-confidence in learning to do more things while being my own boss. Running your own business is prestigious.'

What could be more so than having a beachside apartment in Queensland as your home and work base? 'Working from home allows you to put more capital into your house, money you would otherwise put into your business,' explains author, speaker and cartoonist Andrew Matthews. In this way, he and his wife Julie have been able to justify, in their own minds, spending money on their home. 'Office rent of $500 a week works out to over $25,000 a year,' says Andrew. 'Use that money as 10 per cent of a loan and you have $250,000 to put into your home!'

Andrew has always worked from home, apart from a short period in a picture-framing business at age twenty. Now 39, he believes in 'doing what you love and working hard enough at it so you can keep doing it. If you do what you do for long enough and hard enough, you get the privilege of doing it for a living.'

For Andrew and Julie, this privilege extends to spending their time together. 'We enjoy each other's company so much that it is a bonus to be able to spend the work day with Julie as well as non-working time. She is my partner, my friend and my principal advisor,' says Andrew. That's not to say it is all plain sailing. With no obvious demarcation between work and social life, Andrew has had to learn to stop talking about work at times they have designated, before 8 a.m. and after 6 p.m. And Julie, after being a successful businesswoman in her own right, has decided to step out of the limelight for a while in order to work for Andrew Matthews Productions. Compromises have been made on both sides.

'There is no boss as such, we tend to run the business by consensus,' says Andrew, 'and that can be a slightly difficult thing. You can't give orders to your partner as you would to a stranger that you pay at the end of the week.' Having separate responsibilities eases any tensions. Andrew describes Julie as 'a concepts and ideas person, someone who has the insights and intuitive flashes that change the big picture' while he, 'although not the world's most organised person', is 'a little more in tune with the administration side of things'.

Andrew writes and illustrates books—*Being Happy* and *Making Friends* have been phenomenally successful—speaks publicly and runs the office to a small extent. Julie deals with the sales and marketing side of the business, meticulously arranging their interstate and overseas bookings.

'I grew up with a father who did what he loved and that influenced me,' says Andrew. 'He was a framer, an inventor, a landscape artist and a modest real estate developer. Watching him, I got the impression that work was doing whatever you wanted to do. And if you had to first do something less exciting to support yourself, that gave you even more incentive. I think you need a certain amount of discipline to work from home. And you must love what you do. If you love what you do and you have a vision, then that passion will supply the discipline you need.'

Graphic designer Kym Duval started his own business working from home in 1993. 'A shopfront would only have been marginally more advantageous than word of mouth in attracting work,' he says. 'As for being with other people, I had worked in a team for other companies in the past and being on my own was no deterrent to me.'

He says it takes time to build up a business. Early on, he made some poor financial decisions and charged too little for his services. 'I found I was working long hours—70 to 80 hours a week—for little reward. I work every day, but have cut down to 60 hours now, and find I am most productive at night when there are no disturbances such as the phone ringing.'

As a graphic designer, Kym is involved in 'the artistic arrangement of words and pictures to make the end result as good-looking and powerful as possible'. His projects range from logo designs for corporate identities to stationery and advertisements. He also works on promotional material, which can end up on anything from a T-shirt to the side of a van.

'Some people expect that because you work from home you will be miles cheaper than anyone else. That is not necessarily so. In fact, when you have twenty people working together in a company, you can buy materials in large quantities and offer a cheaper rate, even though the office overheads may be higher. My prices are extremely competitive, but my consumables and utilities obviously still give me a bottom line, so I can't undercut the mainstream business world by a huge margin. It is a hard grind but it's lucky that I like what I do.'

To buy the equipment he needed, Kym took out a bank loan, which he is repaying over ten years. He is happy to be in a situation where everything is under his control. 'I don't have a landlord telling me the rent is going up next week. My costs are fixed and I am now eligible for tax deductions in certain areas.'

'The main advantage for me is being able to spend time with my young family. I'd miss out otherwise, as they would be in bed a few minutes after I had got home from the office.'

'The disadvantage for me is that I am finding it harder and harder to unwind. Even when I am trying to relax, I find myself thinking I should be doing something else. Tight deadlines are the nature of the industry, but I was putting unnecessary pressure on myself to complete work beyond the customer's expectation. Now, I am working out how to cope better with this aspect of my work, so as not to get stressed.'

SUPPORT NETWORKS

Sometimes working from home can be lonely or isolating. With no support and little social contact, minor problems can turn into major difficulties. This is where the assistance and encouragement of organisations such as Home-Based Business Australia can be priceless.

As founder and National Executive Director of this organisation, which began in Victoria, Margaret Seedsman provides services to in excess of 5,000 members nationally. There are networking events throughout the country, which afford members the opportunity to attend regular meetings and breakfast talks. Others benefit from the monthly newsletter. Further useful information is contained in the bimonthly colour magazine *HomeBiz*, aimed specifically at home business and available at newsagencies.

Margaret advises home-based workers on a variety of things:

> People complain that they are being discriminated against, for bank loans, for example. Banks and other institutions are now changing their attitude towards home-based business, as the statistics show this is part of a growing movement. But it will take time to change completely. I tell people that the problem may lie not only in the bank but in how *you* approach the loan application. If you go in apologising for the fact that you are *only* a home-based business, then on some level, you are expecting not to get the loan. And you won't. I believe you create your own reality. If you don't expect it, you don't get it. When I was on the radio recently, a woman called and asked, 'When will people take home-based businesses seriously?' 'When *you* take your home-based business seriously,' I replied. You need to have a professional attitude and feel good about what you do. Be proud of working from home.

Many women partners in home-based businesses feel lonely and isolated, according to Christine Tilley, who is involved with the South Australian chapter of the National Electrical Contractors' Association (NECA). 'Their electrician husbands may be home-based but the men work outside the house,' she says. As a former primary schoolteacher/librarian, Christine was amazed to find there were no support groups when she joined her electrician husband at home. So she became convenor of a network within the South Australian chapter of NECA. The 35 women presently on the register have bimonthly meetings and there is a regular newsletter to keep those who cannot attend informed. 'The role of women is often not recognised,' says Christine. 'They may be directly responsible for the running and management of the business. If they attend trade gatherings they may be made to feel uncomfortable and out of place by the men present. So they can easily miss out on contacts, which can be valuable both socially and to the business.'

The NECA network Christine convened has initiated similar moves in other states. 'We have three aims,' Christine explains: 'to raise the level of awareness of the contribution women make to the electrical industry, to provide a support and social network, and to run courses that can enhance the level of skills in various administrative areas.'

7

DEALING WITH STRESS

Meredith Norman used to be a workaholic. 'In my first job, as a teacher in the country, I found I was spending most evenings and at least one day of the weekend working. I had little time free. I never seemed to be able to relax.' Constantly physically and emotionally on edge, she did not last long. 'By the end of the first term, I had severe tonsillitis and then I ended up in hospital with glandular fever. That told me my body was not coping.'

She tried to change her ways but says, 'If you are a super-conscientious person, as I am, it can be difficult'. Ten years on, nothing had changed. Now teaching at an Adelaide primary school, Meredith would work hard during the week, but it was not uncommon for her to put in additional hours at the weekend. Such commitment naturally took a toll on her physical and emotional health—she suffered from frequent colds and minor ailments—and her social life was limited.

Today, in her home-based homoeopathic business, Meredith applies the lessons she learned as a teacher. She sets aside regular time for outside pursuits and leisure activities ('I play tennis three times a week, have frequent massages and meet with friends often'), she has set a limit to her hours and avoids doing any work on Sundays. 'In my forties I far better understand the importance of a balanced life than I did in my twenties,' she says. 'I am firm about my work times and I pace myself. Having been down the workaholic road and experienced the consequences of stress, I decided that when I started in a new career I would do it differently.'

Stress is a word we hear all too often. 'I feel stressed.' 'I can't cope with all this stress.' 'He's off on stress leave.' But what does it mean? The *Macquarie Dictionary* defines stress as 'a disturbing physiological or psychological influence which produces a state of severe tension in an individual' or, in terms of physics, 'forces on a body which produce a deformation or strain'. In colloquial use, stress is a term covering a wide variety of pressures, social, psychological, work-based and emotional, which produce discomfort or disease when they exceed the body's capacity to cope. When you overstress yourself, your body will manage for a while. But sooner or later, it will start to break down under the strain, putting your well-being at risk.

Stress is not all bad news. Without any stress, without any motivation you would be so relaxed you would be in a coma! Stress is necessary for daily activity, and the right amount of stress keeps us attentive and driven and enables us to perform well. 'I'm looking and feeling ten years younger,' says Philippa Kerslake, who has been running her home-based food business with her partner for several months. It is a taxing and demanding activity that sees her working long hours and travelling interstate to build up new contacts and clients. She admits to feeling anxious and apprehensive at times, yet she is thriving on her new lifestyle. 'Running my own business is the best thing I ever did,' enthuses Philippa, who spent ten years in middle management in large corporations. 'This is so satisfying. We are thrilled and motivated by our achievements.'

Can *you* remember the last time you were pushed to get a piece of work out? Time was desperately short, the client was nagging and insistent and the work was complex and demanding. Yet you did it, somehow. Not only that, but you summoned up all your resources and completed the task to the best of your ability.

How about the time you had to speak in public? Perhaps it was at a work function or at a social event. As you were being introduced, your heart started pounding, your palms felt sweaty and your mouth was suddenly dry. Nothing remarkable in that. Public speaking, after all, rates as one of most people's biggest fears. What *is* remarkable, however, is how your body responded. You felt so charged up with adrenalin that you gave a wonderfully energetic and impassioned speech on the virtues of working at home to a mesmerised audience. 'How did I do it?' you asked yourself afterwards, incredulous at the loud and appreciative applause.

You did it because your body responded to the challenge. Placed in the stressful situation, it went into alert, 'fight or flight' mode. You made a split-second decision whether to stay put and give your talk or take to your heels. Your body snapped into action. Blood was pumped to vital organs and to your muscles as your heart rate increased. Less important functions, such as digestion, slowed down. You started to breathe more quickly and more deeply, taking in more oxygen for immediate energy. Your perspiration rate increased and your body temperature dropped.

The same thing would have happened if you'd chosen to flee. Your body would have prepared you to run as hard and fast as you could. There have been many instances of people being able to perform almost superhuman tasks when under pressure—suddenly leaping over high fences when chased by ferocious dogs or finding themselves able to lift heavy rocks to free a trapped friend.

When John Parker's tractor suddenly reared going up a slope on an isolated NSW opal field, he was thrown clear but his fifteen-year-old daughter Helen was not so fortunate. Her head was jammed between one of the tractor wheels and the trailer behind it. As locals arrived on the scene, someone suggested lifting the tractor to free her. 'I didn't think we could do it,' John admits, 'but we were desperate. Five of us stood under the front of the tractor and, with a mighty grunt, we lifted it about 45 centimetres—making enough space for Helen to be pulled out. It's amazing what you can do when the adrenalin is running.' Due to the prompt action, Helen's life was saved and she went on to make a complete recovery.

The 'fight or flight' response increases our physical capabilities. But when we do neither—and just perservere under constant, unrelenting pressure, neither lashing out nor running away—we maintain that response for hours, days, weeks. And this places enormous stress on our bodies. Our bodies were not designed to stay so alert for prolonged periods. Small wonder we then suffer from ailments such as headaches, backache, frequent colds, an upset stomach and minor illnesses.

Are you too stressed?

Take a few minutes to read through the following questions, answering each one with a 'yes' or 'no.'

1. Do you often suffer from headaches, backache or a sore neck?
2. Do you lose your temper easily?
3. Have you found it hard to make decisions lately?
4. Are you having trouble concentrating at work?
5. When you are not working, do you feel guilty?
6. Have your sleep patterns changed?
7. Have you noticed you are more forgetful recently?
8. Are you unusually irritable, snapping back at people?
9. Do you suddenly find it frustrating to wait in queues?
10. Do you frequently get coughs and colds?
11. Do you find it difficult to relax?
12. Are you drinking more coffee and smoking more cigarettes than usual?
13. Has your alcohol intake increased?
14. Do you find yourself overreacting to minor things?
15. Are you constantly thinking or worrying about work?
16. Do you feel good on a Friday or Saturday (the end of the work week) and bad on a Sunday evening or Monday morning?
17. Is your stomach frequently upset?
18. Does it often feel to you as if your heart is racing?
19. Do you tend to spend more time alone because people have become an irritation?
20. Are you much more impatient and intolerant than you were in the past?

21. Do you feel uneasy in your office or work environment?
22. Do you constantly feel there is not enough time?
23. Do you frequently find yourself daydreaming?

If you answered yes to ten or more of these questions, it would be advisable to look closely at your situation and take action.

Warning signs of stress

Dr Peter Cotton, chair of the Health Issues Advisory Group for the Australian Psychological Society, is a Brisbane clinical psychologist whose special focus is occupational stress. He says that often the earliest sign of stress is disturbed sleep—either difficulty in getting to sleep or waking up in the night and being unable to get back to sleep because one is worrying.

This can progress to other physical signs, says Peter. Common ones are muscle tension leading to headaches and sore neck or backache, pounding heart, dry mouth and sweaty palms, frequent colds and minor illnesses, gastrointestinal disturbances such as upset stomach, fatigue, feeling sick and anxious, and proneness to minor respiratory ailments, coughs and colds and increased allergic reactions.

Stress also has emotional and cognitive effects. The former include impatience, anxiety and irritability. The latter include reduced concentration, forgetfulness and impaired decision making.

Prolonged stress over an extended period can result in raised blood pressure (essential hypertension)—although there is some debate about this—and can contribute to chronic health complaints such as cardiovascular problems, migraines, irritable bowel syndrome and dermatitis.

Stress can result in poor work performance, accidents and ultimately physical collapse. Don't wait until this happens!

Responses to stress

'Your response to stress depends on the sort of person you are,' says Dr Peter Cotton. 'Some people thrive on self-discipline, establishing a routine and getting things done. Others function better where there is some external structure and feel pressurised with deadlines when working alone.'

People also cope with the effects of stress in different ways. Some try to ignore the warning signs, while others try to suppress them. They increase their nicotine, caffeine or alcohol consumption in an attempt to counteract the negative feelings. But all these substances can create a dependency, which brings its own complications. For this reason, they are ineffective long-term solutions.

People usually find they tolerate stress best if they: feel committed to the work they are doing; feel they are being supported in that work; and are receiving adequate remuneration. While you may experience some level of psychological distress and get agitated, you can still function well at work if your morale is high, for example. Once morale drops, though, you will experience the symptoms of stress.

Taking action

'Only you can decide when to take action,' says Dr Cotton. 'It depends on your personality—some recognise the warning signs earlier than others.' There are also gender differences. 'Some women are far more likely to acknowledge the signs and seek help while some men are more likely to turn to coffee, cigarettes or alcohol.'

'By and large, in an ideal world, if your sleep is disturbed on a regular basis, review the situation. Ask yourself what needs to be done. Do not merely take sleeping pills and, when they become ineffective, supplement them with alcohol or demand stronger ones from your doctor. When you have the signs of stress, there is obviously something amiss.'

Ask yourself where the stress is coming from. You may need to alter your work environment in some way, perhaps cutting down on your workload, at least temporarily, or changing your work setting. Alternatively, you may need to increase your personal coping skills.

You may be able to deal with the situation yourself. If not, talk with your doctor. He or she may recommend attending a stress management course—which can help you look at your situation in detail and teach you specific relaxation techniques—or consulting a counsellor or psychologist.

Adelaide GP Dr Alice McLennan says stress is far more likely to adversely affect those who are unable to resolve their situation. 'Someone on the factory floor unable to keep up with the pace of work on the production line and powerless to alter this is *more* prone to the effects of stress than the boss who has responsibility but *control* of 300 staff.'

Margaret Moore, an Adelaide dress designer, loves her teaching job. 'I'm someone who adores people and I gain so much fun and enjoyment from teaching. But the pressure is enormous, it always is in dress design,' she admits. 'You have a big responsibility—to personally supervise every garment for each student.' So, to unwind, she gardens or enjoys her landscape painting.

Physical activity that is in complete contrast to your work is an excellent way to relieve stress. Andrew Matthews plays tennis. 'I get more stressed playing tennis than I do working,' he laughs. 'But having accessible exercise is important to me. I always make sure there is a tennis court where I live, so I can walk off the court at 8 a.m. and be at work by 8.30.'

Jan Somers also strongly believes in the value of having another interest. 'Mine is jogging, and I will take time off to do that no matter what. No matter what deadline I have or where I am, I'll go for a jog some time in the day.'

Adelaide dentist Derick Thomas' solution is not to get stressed in the first place. 'My philosophy is not to work too hard,' he says. 'I see only eight to ten patients a day so that, if a problem develops, I have time to think about it and solve it. But obviously if I had five children to support, I would not have this luxury.' Derick also chooses to work alone, as he has found that strains and tensions are inevitable in any partnership. 'By myself, I'm my own master,' he observes.

'I feel I have got rid of one set of stresses only to replace them with another set,' says Geelong architect Wayne Ketchen, who is married with two young children. 'I no longer have to battle traffic three hours daily, to and from Melbourne, but now I have to find my own jobs, set my own goals, motivate myself, avoid distractions and make enough money to be able to pay the bills at the end of the week.' And, hopefully, make a profit! When it all gets too much, Wayne says, 'I sit down and do some deep breathing. Then I work out my priorities. I manage the crisis.'

That crisis management can take various forms—perhaps a 30-minute walk to clear his head. 'When I return home, I know what I have to achieve.' Wayne also plays badminton weekly and meditates regularly. He became a member of Home-Based Business Australia for networking and for peer support. There, he says, 'You meet people with similar problems which it's good to be able to share and discuss.'

Separating work from non-work

When magazine editor Sue Carney had to temporarily shift her home office to a back room in order to accommodate visitors, she found her output suffered. 'I found it incredibly difficult to get motivated in the living part of the house,' she says, 'and work tended to permeate everywhere.'

A physical separation between work and other aspects of your life is essential both for your general well-being and your work efficiency. If this is not possible at present, plan to create such a separation in the short term. You are making things very hard for yourself from the outset if you attempt to run your home business from the kitchen or living-room table. It *can* be done, it *is* done by some who have no alternative, but this definitely is not a practical long-term situation. The ideal, as we saw in Chapter 3, is to set aside a room or other area specifically for work.

Set clear boundaries between work and non-work. Keep them distinct, so you don't ever find, for example, that you are reading a work document while eating a meal. Working from home, we do not have prompts or cues to structure our day, no set starts or stops. We no longer have to catch the 7.45 a.m. train to arrive at the office by nine. There are no set lunch breaks, morning and afternoon tea times. We have to set our own. Margaret Seedsman knows of one woman who dresses up smartly and comes in through her own front door each morning. She does this to artificially create the beginning of her work day. Another home-based worker, who lives in Sydney, uses breakfast at a local cafe as his start. A short walk in the fresh air, pleasant conversation and a good breakfast set him up for the day ahead.

Sue Carney works at the Sydney office of Reader's Digest two days a week and at home three days a week. 'My working day starts after I drop my two children off at childcare and school. As soon as I re-enter the house, I am in work mode.' She follows office hours and has no problem deciding when to work. 'Once the boys are back, it's impossible to continue,' she laughs.

Others may not have, or want, such a definite end to their working day. Author, cartoonist and speaker Andrew Matthews loves his work so much he could go on and on. 'Sometimes I realise it is four in the afternoon and I have been so engrossed in my drawing I have not even thought of lunch.' Such devotion to work has caused friction between him and his wife, Julie. 'As I don't physically leave my workplace, it is easy to be carrying on after dinner or before breakfast. That can be unfair on Julie,' Andrew says. 'So we have now instituted the rule—that I am not to talk about work after 6 p.m. or before 8 a.m.'

A wise decision, because a balance between work, family life and leisure time is essential. 'Such a balance is the best buffer for stress, the most effective shock absorber,' says Dr Peter Cotton. 'You are far more prone to stress if one or other of these domains is out of balance.'

Dealing with interruptions and distractions

Interruptions can be reduced or kept to a minimum if you have a separate work location. 'I conduct my business from the front room of our house and I get very irate when my bank manager husband comes in on his rostered day off and disturbs me,' says Philippa Kerslake. She is strict about her boundaries. 'I close the door and tell him not to come near me—I don't want any distractions.'

Tell friends and family members who don't live with you that you *work* from home and would prefer not to be contacted during certain hours. Emergencies are, naturally, excluded. I read about one mother who tells her children to disturb her only if the situation is serious, involving lots of smoke or blood and preferably both!

When someone does make a social visit or phone call, there is no need to be brutal and inflexible. Be polite and suggest a more convenient time. And keep the encounter short.

Reader's Digest editor Sue Carney finds she can bend her work hours around interruptions and commitments and hence be *more* productive. 'You might take time off to attend children's school concerts but, working from home, you can still put in a full day's work as your hours are flexible.'

When you work at home, what is there to stop you constantly smoking, raiding the fridge for snacks or drinking endless cups of coffee? Nothing but self-discipline. Here are a few useful tips:

- *Prepare some easy-to-grab snacks.* Put slices of carrot or celery in a bowl of water in the refrigerator. Keep pieces of fruit—apples, pears, bananas—handy. It is far better to snack on fruit and vegetables than on chocolate or biscuits. While sweet snacks may taste good, they provide a quick energy boost followed by a corresponding low when blood sugar levels drop. A good breakfast—cereal and toast—is most important. Complex carbohydrates provide an even release of blood sugar throughout the day.
- *Tackle nicotine cravings.* If you're longing for a cigarette, tell yourself you can have one in 30 minutes, once you have finished your present task. Not only will this increase motivation by giving you something to work towards, but—with a bit of luck—when the 30 minutes have passed, so will your desire for a cigarette. Note the times you automatically reach for a cigarette: with a cup of coffee, at frustrating points in your work, when speaking on the telephone. Make a point of disregarding these cues.
- *Limit daily coffee intake* by substituting other drinks—tea, hot chocolate, water. Note that a cup of coffee contains about 240 mg of caffeine, while a cup of tea contains just 80 mg.

Television can be another addictive distraction. 'If the TV is on at lunchtime for the rest of the family, I watch with them,' says Wayne Ketchen, 'and before I know it, much time has gone by.' Be strong. Avoid daytime television. It is all too easy to get hooked.

The view indoors

One of the reasons you chose to work from home may be your pleasant and peaceful surroundings. Perhaps you are fortunate enough, like Sue Carney, to have a spectacular view in the Blue Mountains. Or maybe you work in a tropical setting, overlooking an expanse of unspoilt beach and palm trees in Darwin. But what about the view *indoors*—the dirty plates in the sink you notice every time you make yourself a coffee, the overflowing laundry basket in the bathroom and the dirty kitchen floor?

'I just ignore it,' says Sue Carney. 'In an office you can shut yourself away from all that. You are cut off from home and personal life. Here it is staring you in the face all the time.'

And calling out to you! Sometimes it can seem far more appealing to scrub out a filthy saucepan than to apply yourself to completing that set of house drawings. Disregard the call. Be strong and discipline yourself. After all, what would you rather have at the end of the week or month—a pay packet or a clean house?

With a little organisation, it is possible to incorporate some household chores into your work day. After sitting in front of the computer screen for an hour—at most—loosen up your muscles by putting a load of washing on. As long as you have short, limited breaks, you can make circumstances work *for* you rather than *against* you. Short breaks can actually promote concentration and increase productivity.

'I love what I do,' says Melbourne desktop publisher Maggie Boday, 'but I also like the house to be tidy. I can overlook the dirty dishes and the unmade beds, I don't fuss over that, but I would like to get someone in to do the ironing.' And why not? That could let her make more money, and save her sanity in the process!

If you pay someone $20 each week to do ironing that would take you two hours, and your time is charged at $40 an hour, you don't have to be a mathematical genius to figure out what makes better financial sense. Forget about the guilt you may feel. Look at the added bonus—by hiring someone, you are creating a job!

Look at changing your priorities and even lowering your standards. Concentrate on keeping just *one* part of the house smart and presentable: the area where you see clients.

Coping with children

'I have a brilliant idea and I'm tapping away at the computer when a voice says, "Mum, I'm hungry". You get this interference all the time and while you *can* stop to make a sandwich, there are times when you just don't want to,' says real estate adviser and writer Jan Somers.

Isn't it ironic? One of the reasons you chose to work from home was so you could spend more time with the family. Now that very same family is driving you to distraction—the baby is bawling, the youngsters are back from school and demanding your attention. Meanwhile you are trying your hardest to concentrate on a major report for an important client, due tomorrow.

The key to your plight is organisation, coupled with a little flexibility and common sense. Look closely at your circumstances.

'You have to be fair on the children,' advises Jan. 'Mine are fairly good and understand there is a work ethic in the house. And I make sure I pull myself away from work to give them talk time, perhaps 30 minutes each night. I don't have a strict regime—that's the good thing about working from home, you *can* take time off. My husband and I have made a commitment—that we *will* take time off to do things with the children, such as going to their sports carnivals. It's not like when you are working for someone else and you say, "I'm sorry, I can't get down there, those are my work hours."'

Some people set strict guidelines. Others, like Jan, are more flexible. Consider the age of your children. You can't possibly hope to work effectively at a demanding home business if you are also having to provide total care for a toddler. Don't fool yourself that you can, and don't waste your time trying. Some companies go so far as to prohibit their employees from doing home-based work unless alternative childcare arrangements have been made.

Aside from registered childcare centres, you may be able to call on your partner or a relative to help out here. Sue Carney is fortunate in both respects. Her two boys attend childcare and school on the days she works from home, and husband Paul looks after them on the days she is at the office. Paul is a journalist who has opted for part-time work in order to be able to do this. Both partners are happy with the arrangement. Sue does not worry about her sons, as she knows they are in good hands. 'I'm only ten minutes' drive away from childcare, so I can be there almost immediately if anything happens to them.'

Architect Wayne Ketchen works full time in his home office while his wife, Joanne, cares for 18-month-old Madison and four-and-a-half-year-old Alexander. 'Joanne gave up her teaching job two years ago, so I am now the primary income-earner. While she was still working, my mother-in-law looked after Alexander,' Wayne explains. 'One of the biggest disadvantages in working from home is being accessible to the kids. "Daddy" is always there. I am reluctant to say, "My hours are nine till five so don't disturb me". Instead I'll take fifteen minutes off and make up that time elsewhere. It's come as a surprise to me that one of the advantages of working from home—being able to spend more time with the family—can also be a disadvantage. Yet it's a valuable experience watching the children grow up, and I am always there to help.'

With older children, it's a different story. Jan Somers involves her youngsters in her work, which she thinks helps teach them the importance of the work ethic and the value of money. 'I try to include them without being pushy. My older son has become interested and he'll ask, "What can I do to earn a Slurpee today, Mummy?" So I'll give him a bundle of brochures that need stapling. I do this to teach my children the discipline of business and to help them understand how business works.'

Errands and chores

'When I first started working from home, Peter would say things like "If you get a moment, could you vacuum this or dust that?" as he left for his bank job in the morning. He would talk about the time I first "gave up work"—yet I now work longer and harder at home than I ever did!' laments Philippa Kerslake.

'People assume that if you are at home, you are available to run errands,' says telecommuting consultant Paul Chung. It takes a while to adjust—your partner, children and friends need to be made aware that they can't ask you to pick up the dry-cleaning. You would not be able to do this if you were working in a city office, so what is so different now? Carry out chores in your breaks or else do them outside working hours.

Routine

Without a realistic set of tasks assigned for the day, you can find time drifting by without your achieving anything. Look at your *productivity* rather than your *activity.* It is easy to keep busy, but harder to be effective. Speaker Andrew Matthews says, 'I evaluate myself at the end of each day and ask myself, "What have I achieved today?" If at the end of the day I have not made some impression, I put in a few more hours.' Andrew's attitude is: 'If you love what you do and you have a vision, then that passion will supply the discipline you need.'

Unfortunately, for most of us passion is not quite enough. We need a working structure as well. For a start, it is sensible to define your working hours—both times when you are actually working and other times when you make yourself available to clients. Adelaide dentist Derick Thomas works in his surgery five days a week and can be contacted after hours for emergencies. Homoeopath Meredith Norman makes herself available for 45 hours a week, 'but I do not have personal contact with clients all that time'.

Dr David Kavenagh, former head of the Department of Psychology at Sydney University and now Associate Professor, Department of Psychiatry at the University of Queensland, says defining work hours 'helps with the guilt many people experience when they are not working'. He suggests routinely setting aside leisure time—'from 4 p.m. to 5 p.m., play with my daughters'. 'That sounds hard and cynical but it provides you with permission to do so,' he says. 'It is written in your diary, so you can say "I'm not available for the meeting—I have something on at four." ' Of course, he adds, you should not plan *all* your leisure time—'that too can be stressful. But do plan to have regular time off, pursuing a hobby, perhaps visiting the theatre, playing sport.'

David Kavenagh has found that most people working from home are highly motivated—they have, after all, chosen to work in this way—so for them the problem is far more likely to be *stopping* work than *starting* it.

Two words about guilt—*forget it.* Guilt is an appalling waste of energy and a drain on your resources. Instead, set realistic aims each work day, and take regular breaks. 'If you work at an outside location, there is preparation and unwinding time,' Dr Kavenagh explains. 'You have to travel there. I listen to more classical music driving to and from work than at any other time. That gives me great pleasure and calms me. You miss that working from home, so give yourself permission to sit and listen to music for ten minutes. This can be very helpful in terms of promoting concentration. To get to the train station, you may have had to walk up and down stairs. That can help concentration as well as fitness. So take an active break from sitting in front of the computer or doing a long task. You will find your productivity rises!'

'You need to set yourself a schedule or else the day is a mess,' agrees Jan Sutherland of Dial-A-Wife Cleaning Services. 'I just run around in circles and get nowhere.' Jan has taken to writing down the six tasks she wants to achieve in the day and finds this very helpful. 'Ideally I'd do this the night before and put them down in order of priority. I handle at least four and put the rest down on the next day's sheet.'

Why bother writing it down? 'I know exactly what I aim to do,' you may tell yourself. But committing your tasks to paper will clarify them and make them concrete entities. Prioritising them and ticking them off as you go along will provide you with a sense of achievement. You will find yourself becoming much more efficient.

Business worries

American author Mark Twain once remarked that he had been through some terrible things in his life, some of which had actually happened. What an accurate observation, and yet how difficult it is to avoid worrying.

There you are, working on an order or project but already focusing on the next piece of work. What if there is *no* next piece of work? If your business is not going well, this can be a real concern. How will you survive financially? How will you pay your bills, feed yourself and your family, keep the mortgage going . . .? Before you know it, you have worked yourself into a frantic state of mind. So much so that you can no longer concentrate on the task in hand.

Stop right now! Say to yourself, 'I have a problem to solve but I will not think about it right now. I'll do that at 5 o'clock today.' Having set this time aside, you can stop dwelling on the problem and instead concentrate on the task in hand. By the time 5 o'clock arrives, your 'problem' may already be solved. Perhaps a client has called with the offer of more work. Perhaps a large cheque has come in the mail to pay off an outstanding debt. Perhaps three prospective clients have called in response to your newspaper advertisement.

By the time 5 o'clock arrives, you may be breathing a sigh of relief. But, if nothing has changed since the morning, you now have some free time—not so much for worrying as to think about practical steps to increase business or to solve your problem. *Why* has there been a slump in business? Do you need to advertise more widely? Are your costs and charges too high? Perhaps a talk with your accountant is in order. Setting aside the time to concentrate on your concerns pushes the worry aside. Taking action can banish it altogether.

Being a Jack of all trades

Working from home, you are likely to be working alone and hence wearing all the hats for your business. As well as doing the work you enjoy—as a photographer, electrician or computer consultant—you also need to be receptionist, bookkeeper, and secretary. You need to deal with client enquiries, type letters, send out invoices and keep track of accounts. You need to make the coffee, do the filing, collect and post the mail and so on. Little wonder it seems there are not enough hours in the day.

You are under a tremendous amount of pressure. So make it as easy for yourself as possible. Relieve that pressure wherever you can. Learn to delegate. We all have our strengths and weaknesses, and it is a rare individual who is a happy and competent all-rounder. If you loathe the bookwork or can't manage the typing and find they cause you hours of misery, why not hire someone to do them for you? A professional may take half the time. Meanwhile you can put your hours to better use generating an income by doing what you are good at, whether it be painting, designing houses or drilling teeth. Another thing to bear in mind is to be well-organised. Time spent searching for that elusive but vital piece of paper is wasted time. Make setting up an efficient filing system a top priority.

Take a morning off to look at your own situation in detail and ask how you can save yourself time and effort. 'Many businesses fail because their owners have too many hats to wear,' says Jan Sutherland of Dial-A-Wife Cleaning Services. 'Not only do they have to perform many different functions, they may also have no skills or experience in them.' Jan has had to deal with administration and warehousing, finances, secretarial duties, sales and marketing. 'You stumble as you learn. While you may have the natural aptitude and intelligence for these tasks, they can drag you down. You have to do all this *as well as* your work, which can be all-encompassing. These tasks can stop you being effective.'

Jan has found two solutions work for her—delegation and paying for professional services. Since her husband, Ross, joined her in the business, the couple have divided up the tasks. 'I do not enjoy the paperwork so he does that and all the bookkeeping. I prefer to train the staff.' They have also put aside capital to employ a business mentor. 'He can look at our business in a different way,' says Jan, 'provide a fresh new outlook and advise us.' A professional, objective overview has led them to focus on their objectives rather than waste time taking unprofitable directions. 'We put our marketing plan to him and he brought us back to reality,' laughs Jan. Ross adds: 'He told us, "You are working all these hours for *this* much money. You would be far better off financially working *for* someone." Well, we knew that. Everyone tends to go into their own business looking through rose-coloured glasses. It's a hard slog, but we have a vision and we're prepared to gamble to reach it.'

With the help of their business mentor, the Sutherlands studied their business plan once more and made changes. 'Our priorities shifted after twelve months—to concentrating on expanding the business, training cleaners rather than doing the cleaning ourselves. That also left us time to develop cleaning products,' says Ross.

The meaning of work

As we have seen, work offers far more than the financial means to survive. It gives one a sense of identity, a feeling of purpose, and social contact. And, however much you may moan about the tedium of your present job and the accompanying office politics, it is important to consider the absence of such factors as you prepare to work from home.

While you may harbour the fantasy that a life without work would be ideal, remind yourself this *is* just a fantasy. Sooner or later lottery winners become bored, retirees lose motivation and the unemployed suffer low self-esteem and become despondent. The reality is that life without work, whether this happens by choice or circumstance, can be an unhappy existence.

It is worth looking in more detail at one Australian who discovered the truth of this statement. Jan Somers as good as won the lottery with her shrewd investments in real estate over the years. By the time she was 37, she had given up her high school teaching career. After all, she was a millionaire and had no need to work. Or so she thought. For, after a few years at home with the children, she found she lacked the mental stimulation gainful employment had given her. Although she had other interests, there was a limit to how far she could indulge herself. 'I derive great enjoyment from jogging,' she says. 'I jogged every day of my three pregnancies, until each child was born. Jogging kept me fit but I needed more than that. I might have had all the time in the world but I wanted to keep my mind fit as well as my body.'

Believing that 'to rest is to rust', she set herself personal goals. After realising that selling real estate was not for her, she set about writing down what she had learnt about property investment. Both real estate agents and lay investors snapped up her 56-page booklet, and she realised there could be a market for her knowledge.

Jan's first self-published book sold 200,000 copies—an outstanding success in Australian publishing, where sales of 7,000 qualify a book as a best-seller—and her subsequent books have proved equally popular. Jan finds her new life rewarding and fulfilling, enjoyable and great fun. And after all, isn't that what life is all about? She travels interstate regularly to give seminars and puts together supporting computer software packages with her husband, who left his government job to join her. Their business is booming.

Jan looked at what she enjoyed doing—teaching and passing on what she had learnt to others. 'It would be wonderful for everyone to be financially independent,' she says, 'and with investment in real estate, that is possible.'

Unemployment

Flinders University psychology professor Norman Feather is well aware that work contributes to social, psychological and economic well-being. His research on the unemployed has found that both lack of structure and purpose in one's life and lack of finance can cause unhappiness. 'We need goals and purpose,' he says. 'A salary may be the manifest aspect of work, but employment also offers the opportunity for the use of one's skills, social contact, variety and activity. Working from home you would still be exercising these skills and earning an income, but you may miss out on social contact.'

The problems of professional and social isolation are discussed in detail in Chapter 8. 'Unemployed people can become depressed and lose self-esteem,' continues Professor Feather. 'They may indulge in passive behaviour such as watching television and sleeping in.'

'For the majority of people, work is part of identity,' says Professor Trevor Parmenter of the Unit for Community Integration Studies at Sydney's Macquarie University. 'It defines who you are to the public and to yourself, your self-identity. And this is of great importance.' The loss of a job can be devastating. 'I have heard of men who are retrenched and continue to get up at the same time, catch the same train with their packed lunch and not tell their wife. They feel humiliated at losing their job, they feel helpless and hopeless.'

So it seems that many of us *need* work if we are to enjoy a reasonable quality of life.

Through his work with disabled people, Professor Parmenter has concluded that work can perhaps be too highly emphasised as a determinant of social worth. He is critical of this. 'Nevertheless,' he says, 'for some people, work is the main thing on which their whole life hinges. I have come across disabled people who have told me "We like working in real jobs" rather than sheltered workshops. "It shows we have more value, people respect us more, we know who we are." That may well be the case for some. I have met a couple, both in wheelchairs, running a motel to provide accommodation for disabled people.' Working from home can be an ideal solution for disabled people.

Retirement

Professor Sol Encel is the co-author, with Helen Studencki, of *Retirement: A Survey*, published by the NSW Consultative Committee on Ageing. He has found that early retirement can be a threat to health, wealth and a sense of well-being. 'Activity is the best guarantee of good health and life satisfaction,' he says. 'My research demonstrates that the best assurance of good health after retirement is to work—whether that is voluntary or not.' The reason for this is that work is so central to daily life. 'Losing your daily routine, life shape and social networks can have a bad effect on many people. I've spoken to doctors who have patients who have left work and would like to go back but can't. They feel frustrated with life and are being treated for depression and minor illnesses.' It would be far better if people did not have to retire or chose when they wanted to. A large percentage of people aged 50 to 65 appear to be retired but are really chronically unemployed—no employer would take them on at that age.

'We need to get away from the notion that a gate closes behind you when you retire—it is not like that.' Indeed, working from home can be an ideal next step. John Ehm (see page 21) started up Homechain, his home-based accommodation business for tourists, after he was laid off at age 60. 'I had taken on a builder-trainer position in an Aboriginal community north of Cairns, but the job was made redundant midway through the five-year contract,' John explains. Having rented out their Brisbane home, he and his wife, Emmy, decided to settle in Cairns, where two of their daughters and six grandchildren lived.

John now faced a dilemma. He needed an income, but 'Who would employ a 60-year-old in 1992?' he asked himself. He considered his options and his interests. For John, these included travel—visiting cattle stations and properties—and meeting people. 'Elderly people need to keep busy—a man's life expectancy is now 80 or 90. And I have grandchildren who will need jobs. There is a high unemployment rate in Cairns. By creating a business, I can employ them and others. My long-range plan is to help pensioners—to have them open their homes to tourists for friendship and for finance.'

Professor Encel has spoken to some who have accepted redundancy packages. 'Early retirement is a bit of an illusion,' he comments. 'You think you are going to be financially secure, but that is often not the case. The economic situation can worsen, interest rates drop and suddenly the package you were offered is not so attractive. You may have unexpected calls on your money, due to illness, or you may need to help out your unemployed children. So if your present job is boring, stressful or physically unhealthy, would it not be better to change it or go into a different career altogether?'

Working from home makes sense under these circumstances because:

- Removal of work can have a bad effect on you as you lose your daily routine and life shape, social networks and contacts.
- Your money may turn out to be insufficient when you retire.
- Thirty years of leisure can be tedious. With current long life expectancies, retirement can last 30 years.

Professor Encel practises what he preaches. Having retired from full-time teaching seven years ago, he says he has never been busier. He works as a researcher at the University of New South Wales' Social Policy Research Centre. This is unpaid work; his income comes from consulting work.

'For the minority of retirees, retirement is leisure,' he says. 'But that is only for a minority. Giving up work suddenly and without preparation is not advisable. There is a definite phenomenon of premature death after retirement. Unfortunately, we only hear of the dramatic occurrences—people dropping dead eighteen months after retiring. No accurate surveys have been done, but this does happen,' he says.

Here is yet another reason for easing into a home-based business gradually. If you are thinking of working from home, *prepare* for it. Do not launch yourself into it suddenly. This can be unwise for a number of reasons, not least of which is sudden fluctuation in income. And bear in mind—if you *enjoy* what you are doing, as Jan Somers and John Ehm do, you are far more likely to be successful.

One of the most inspiring individuals Professor Encel has come across in his research is a 71-year-old woman living in a Melbourne retirement village. 'She works as a copy editor for magazines, using telephone, fax and mail facilities. She jokes that she is glad to do it that way, at a distance, so no one knows her age. This woman is very effective working from home. All domestic responsibilities are seen to by the retirement village. Her husband is long since dead. Her children live far away, but not seeing them frequently does not bother her. She is happy and fulfilled in the lifestyle she has created for herself.'

REVIEW

Stress results in physical, emotional and cognitive effects.

Reduce the effects of stress by:

- physically separating work and living areas;
- setting core work times;
- making a daily schedule—listing several tasks in order of priority and ticking off each one as completed;
- limiting interruptions to work by setting your limits from the outset and discouraging social visits and telephone calls in work time;
- snacking on pre-prepared fruit and vegetables rather than sugar-rich foods;
- taking regular breaks and having proper, well-balanced meals;

- cutting down on cigarettes;
- substituting tea, hot chocolate or water for coffee;
- unplugging the television;
- incorporating small domestic chores into your work day for a physical and emotional interval;
- setting your organised, but flexible, work schedule around your children;
- putting aside time to solve any work problems; and
- delegating or paying for professional services such as bookkeeping.

Recommended reading

If you are interested in learning more about stress and how to deal with it, there are many excellent books on the topic, among them:

You and Stress—A Guide to Successful Living, by Dr Bob Montgomery and Lynette Evans, Melbourne, Victoria, Nelson, 1984

Coping with Stress, by Dr Bob Montgomery, Melbourne, Victoria, Pitman, 1982

Managing Stress—The Stress Survival Guide for Today, by Ursula Markham, Dorset, United Kingdom, Element, 1989 (published in Brisbane, 1995)

Stress—How Your Diet Can Help, by Stephen Terrass, London, United Kingdom, Thorsons, 1994

Amanda Gore's Stress Buster, Sydney, New South Wales, Lifestyle Press, 1991

The Relaxation & Stress Reduction Workbook, by Martha Davis, Elizabeth Robbins Eshelman and Matthew McKay, Oakland, California, New Harbinger Publications, 1995

IN SICKNESS AND IN HEALTH

When illustrator Rod Hutchison fell down some slippery steps, he was thankful he had not injured his right, drawing, hand. But he did not feel quite so pleased to discover he had broken his left arm. 'I was completely unable to work for four weeks and only on a part-time basis for the following three weeks,' he says. Fortunately he was covered by the loss-of-income insurance he had taken out some time previously. This, however, did not take effect for two weeks. Even then, it provided him with enough to cover only his household expenses, not even to run a car. Such insurance can come into play earlier, or later, than the two-week period Rod had selected. The weekly payout can also be higher, but for that you will need to pay a higher premium and Rod reckons the $400 a year he pays now is high enough. 'I had a bit of money to tide me over but I found I had to dip into my capital to keep going.' Just as well—for he received his cheque from the insurance company almost three months after the event!

'I was making real estate sketches for a client at the time of the accident,' Rod says, 'and I will now be lodging a claim against the household insurance of the owner.'

Rod's experience shows the necessity for home-based workers to have such income protection insurance and sufficient health insurance. He now considers it vital to look after your health and to keep fit.

'I had a heart attack last Christmas and I'm sure it was partly caused by work pressures. The computerisation of newspapers has resulted in shorter deadlines. Where once I had to deliver my real estate sketches by midday Friday for them to be published in Saturday's newspaper, they now have to be in by Thursday. Sometimes advertising agencies even require them by Wednesday, which makes life very difficult for me and makes me very tense.

'Mine is mainly a sedentary job. I spend a lot of time finishing the sketches at my desk. Sometimes I'll have huge weeks, working from 6 a.m. to 10 p.m., putting in 70-hour weeks. Most of the time I will work 50 hours a week. I'm working in a fiercely competitive industry with a lot of people fighting over a finite number of customers. A lot of people can draw houses, and they undermine the market by doing very cheap work. Luckily for me it is not of good quality, and they don't last. The recession also shook out quite a few people. You build up clients through loyalty and goodwill and by doing the job on time. You can ruin an entire weekend for a real estate agent—if you don't complete the drawings, they cannot put together their brochure or catalogue.'

Having a heart attack made Rod reassess his fitness level and work style. 'I now do a lot of walking and I have learnt to meditate,' he says.

When one has chronic health problems, working from home can be a convenient option. Sue, the business partner and wife of electrician Bob Flaherty, suffers from an autoimmune disease. Yet Bob considers Sue's contribution invaluable. 'She is the heart of the business,' he says. 'Sue is able to deal with customers over the telephone, help sort out any problems and take care of the finances—organising the accounts and bookkeeping on the home computer. Sometimes her help can be restricted because of the disease, but we work round that.'

'Bob loves his work and I get a buzz out of it,' says Sue. 'With my condition, I could not hold down a job. I have constant muscle and joint pain and it is very tiring. It can be difficult to be pleasant with customers at times—the calls start at 6 a.m. and sometimes don't stop until 10 o'clock—and you need to be aware of the *real* emergencies, whatever the customer insists!'

After sixteen years, Sue has got used to the lifestyle. 'It has become like a second skin. Your life is not your own most of the time,' she explains. Adding to the pressure is the fact that Bob and Sue's 25-year-old daughter, Jane, suffers from the same autoimmune disease. 'It is thought to be hereditary, affects mainly women, can be treated but there is no cure,' Sue explains. Jane had to give up work. She now suffers from daily migraines and is practically confined to bed—another reason why working outside the house would not be possible for Sue. 'We are a happy family, though, we don't go around with long faces,' she says cheerfully. 'Our 27-year-old son Christopher also lives at home with us. He doesn't want to leave—so we must be doing something right!'

Others thrive in a home setting. 'I have been sick a lot less at home than in the office,' says journalist Paula Ruzek, who now specialises in publication production. 'When I worked for *Business Review Weekly*, I had five colds, one after the other. That was from travelling on public transport and from airconditioning in the building. I'd feel I had just got over one cold when the next one would start. Now I get one cold a year at most. I'm extremely healthy. I go for walks and to the gym, as I always did. But now I can choose my times, and go to the gym in the morning rather than the evening.'

WAYS WITH WORDS

'Today was a good example of why I work from home,' says writer Libby Gleeson. 'One of my daughters injured her arm a week ago but she left it until today, the first day of the school term, to say it was hurting. So we spent two hours in the X-ray department at the hospital. Luckily nothing was broken, it was a sprained wrist.

'Working from home gives me flexibility and independence. I can deal with the domestic situation, if someone is sick, and I can attend committee meetings such as for the Sydney Writers' Festival and at my children's school. I find working much less stressful now. Whether that is because I am doing what I love or working from home, I don't know.'

Libby has a teaching background and has worked at the Institute of Languages at the University of New South Wales, training others to teach English as a second language. Today she is known for her children's books, such as *Love Me, Love Me Not*, *Where's Mum?* and *Hannah Plus One*. She was able to combine teaching and writing for four years, until her third child was born. 'Then something had to give,' she explains, 'and that proved to be my teaching career.'

She believes that, working from home, you need to make certain decisions. 'You are going to be a worker, this is your job. You have to decide whether that job will be full-time or part-time.'

For writer and GP Peter Goldsworthy, the job is part-time. He works at home in the morning, on his poems, books and scripts, and then heads off to his wife Helen's medical practice in the afternoon.

'It's better that way,' he says. 'With writing, I run out of steam by lunchtime and I get bored—unless something is going, like the second or third draft of a novel, and then I resent having to leave. But more often than not, it is a nice respite.'

Peter has worked part-time in medicine ever since he graduated. 'I looked after the children and worked part-time while Helen completed her studies. It would have been impossible for both of us to be studying.' He has been writing for seventeen years, winning national and international literary awards in the process. His first novel, *Maestro*, is a set text for Year 12 in several states and is now on CD-ROM. His books of poetry and short-story collections are highly acclaimed, some posing controversial questions, such as whether higher animals have feelings similar to those of humans, as in his novel *Wish*.

He works at home in a small office which he describes as 'a sparse little convent room'. 'I believed some discomfort was necessary,' he explains. His computer faces the wall. A printer and fax machine are placed on either side and a window is on his right. 'I don't want too good a view, otherwise I would get distracted. I know of writers who have rented an office to overcome distractions. I tend to give way to them. I work in one-hour blocks and then have a coffee or something to nibble. Film scripts are different—they have deadlines and that is quite useful.'

Jenny Church of Your Type Secretarial Services is used to dealing with deadlines. To her, they are a lifestyle. The demands placed on her by clients with short deadlines are such that she feels she will never have enough time. 'But I cope, I have always lived like that. I am trying to learn the violin to relax,' she says, 'and that is very enjoyable.'

With over 25 years' experience behind her—as an executive secretary and office manager of a legal practice—Jenny was well-qualified to set up her home-based secretarial business in 1989. Nevertheless, she regrets 'going in cold'. 'Although I knew the field fairly well, I should have taken the building-up time into consideration. I had no business plan then, but I'm looking at one seriously now. With hindsight, it would have been wise to have done this initially. You can be so busy there is no time to ask yourself where you are heading, what you are doing or what you should be doing. And soon you may be wasting money in certain areas or not costing things properly or having to work at too rapid a rate in order to get things done.

'I advertise in the *Yellow Pages* but I have found the best advertising is by word of mouth. It took me about eighteen months to build up the business and, had I been depending on the income, I would have starved. My husband was still working then—he is now retired.'

She believes in getting and keeping repeat business. 'I've seen work that has been grossly overcharged. You can sell anything *once*. It is regular customers that count.'

Relationships are another important consideration. 'Working at home can cause friction with my husband,' Jenny admits. 'He'll say "You've messed up two rooms, you may as well ruin the rest." He resents the space my work has taken.' Jenny's office is at the front of the house. Clients come through the front door and into an area set up as a waiting room. Work time can also cause conflicts. 'My husband gets upset when I can't get away for weekends at 3 p.m. Sometimes I'll be tied up until 6 o'clock.

'How do I placate him? I go on my merry way,' she laughs. 'He helps, getting the mail and paying accounts, things I would not otherwise get round to. He will make me a coffee, he has taken over the household duties. Now that he is retired, he keeps himself busy with his shell collection. He does not interrupt me or my work. You have to set the ground rules—this is a job, not something you do for play or for pin money. Working from home is what I do for a living.'

In Melbourne, Pamela and Gary LaPersonne earn their income at home, from the topic of working from home! Gary is the founding editor of *HomeBiz*, Australia's first magazine for and about home businesses, and his wife Pamela deals with the associated marketing and promotion. *HomeBiz* started as an eight-page newsletter in February 1994 with a circulation of 500. Today it is a 36-page colour magazine sold nationally through newsagencies and circulation has swelled from 500 to 10,000.

Pamela sees herself as fairly typical of home-based workers. 'I started working from home twenty years ago, after I had my first son. I bought an electric typewriter from my former employer and started my own typing business, advertising at the TAFE college and universities. I also contacted local architects because I had worked in an architectural office. Now we have four computers (including a high-powered Mac), printers, fax, copiers, modem—the works. While there are still people starting out like I did, things are a lot more serious now. There is much more competition.'

Pamela did well when she started in her business but was troubled by the notion that being home-based she was not taken seriously. 'It all seemed too easy to be a real business. Then I did a stupid thing and bought an established secretarial service, taking on an expensive lease in commercial premises. I subsequently added a personnel consultancy.' When she started a newsletter to promote the businesses, the response was so great that she and Gary realised they had tapped a market. The couple set up their own publishing business, the Wise Group, and Gary left his position as deputy editor at *New Idea* to work from home. Persuaded to return, his services are now retained on contract by the magazine.

As for many others, working from home has provided the La Personnes with flexibility. 'The best thing I ever did was leave the secretarial service and come home,' says Pamela. 'Someone asked me the other day, what I would do—working from home—if I wanted to be in the garden. I replied, "I can be!" I moved the business home because my three-year-old son Deke, who would come into the office with me, had become curious and extremely mobile. While I was occupied with a client on the phone he would escape through the front door and disappear in moments. Once, I found him on the seventh floor—he had climbed up a staircase that consisted only of concrete slabs without a railing. I thought that was diabolical. The real reason working from home took off was because of mothers staying at home with the children. People who work from home do so for the lifestyle. We are unpretentious, we do not want the glamour and glitz of the office. *HomeBiz* is the same—unpretentious and flexible. We are in very close contact with our readers and tailor the magazine to their needs. Larger organisations cannot do this, but we are able to instantly respond—bringing in the subjects readers want, doing sales and marketing, connecting to the Internet. We did what we tell our readers to do, we took the same advice. We started small and grew in a controlled manner.'

8

MAKING IT WORK

Once your business is up and running, certain unexpected 'problems' may arise. This chapter reviews and expands on topics touched on earlier. By considering those 'problems' as challenges and tackling them head-on, you can improve both your work situation and your lifestyle, and help create a rich and fulfilling existence for yourself.

Social isolation

After years of thinking and planning, I found myself in my ideal situation—being paid for what I enjoy doing most of all, writing. This was not *work* to me. This was a joy and a pleasure—being paid to interview fascinating people, read intriguing books and talk with their authors afterwards. Yet there was one aspect of my new life that I had not anticipated: social isolation.

Sure, much of the time I was out and about interviewing. I was by no means alone. But even if I did join British actress

Hayley Mills in a cup of coffee or watch other tennis champions practising while I chatted with John Fitzgerald, this was not the same as contact with friends and work colleagues. I found that I really missed these social interactions. I began to appreciate that my old job had many positive aspects: the stimulating exchange of ideas, the light banter and laughs and, above all, the company. Working alone, I found it all too easy to get bogged down, take everything too seriously, and become obsessed with work.

I found I had to initiate social contact far more than before. I would meet friends occasionally for lunch or, more frequently, for a cup of coffee. I found this gave me a boost in my work because it eased my isolation. Naturally I had to keep time in mind—just an hour at most for lunch, and a short coffee break. But all of my friends were working as well, so their time, too, was limited.

Sydney writer Libby Gleeson, who previously worked as a teacher, finds that not having work colleagues nearby is both an advantage and a disadvantage. 'You are not involved in office politics or competing against one another so that a 9 to 5 job becomes a 9 to 7 one,' she explains. 'But the downside is that, when you feel like going out to relax, you find that your friendship circle has shrunk because you are no longer seeing people day to day. Many of the writers I know live outside Sydney, so we keep our friendship going by means of telephone calls and occasional visits.'

Dr David Kavenagh, Associate Professor in the Department of Psychiatry, University of Queensland, has worked from home for part of each week. 'I find the use of e-mail extremely rewarding,' he says. He uses the Internet to keep in contact with his professional colleagues interstate and in the United Kingdom. 'I felt as if I was talking to them. It was like exchanging letters but almost immediate. It was serious work as well as socialising.'

Many home workers who have face-to-face encounters with clients find that, eager for social contact, they spend longer chatting with them than they would do otherwise.

Beware of becoming socially isolated and make the effort to catch up with friends.

Professional isolation

Working alone, you can easily get out of touch with your trade or profession. What new developments have been made? What new products are on the market? Where is your business or industry headed? If you find you no longer know the answers, the solution is simple:

Join professional bodies and organisations, subscribe to newsletters and journals and initiate regular meetings with colleagues.

I am a member of the Australian Journalists Association Section of the Media, Entertainment and Arts Alliance, the Australian Society of Authors, the South Australian Writers' Centre and Home-Based Business Australia. I buy *HomeBiz* magazine and I have also kept up my dental registration, which gives me the option of delving into mouths when I tire of minds!

'I have made a point of joining the Chamber of Commerce and the Australian Marketing Institute so I can meet other people,' says Julie Matthews. 'It can get claustrophobic working from home.'

Home-based organisational psychologist Bruce Crowe warns that when you network on an informal basis, 'You [and the others] may be competing for the same business'. Meetings at professional organisations and associations, being on neutral ground, are preferable, he says.

Loss of social status and self-esteem

'It was hard at first for me to work for Andrew Matthews Productions with my husband,' admits Julie Matthews. 'I had had my own company—a modelling and finishing school—with thirteen staff members. I was used to having things done for me—others made my coffee or went to the post office for me. They did the more menial jobs while I got on with running the business, keeping them happy working as a team, doing my own job *and* bringing in money to pay them.'

Julie found that, working with and essentially for Andrew, she lost some status. 'It was a big compromise for both of us,' she says. 'Andrew sold his company—he was running his own seminars—and we started working together. I am in the background, as I market Andrew and his talks and seminars. But I also like speaking and sharing my knowledge, so I also do that to a certain extent, teaching business etiquette and corporate grooming. But Andrew is in the limelight now. I've been there and enjoyed it. Once Andrew is settled in, I will go back to it.'

When Ross Sutherland left teaching to join his wife Jan in Dial-A-Wife cleaning services, he experienced no loss in social status. 'It's funny, but I would get a quiet sense of satisfaction going to work in a dirty house for three or four hours and seeing an instantaneous reward for my efforts. That does not happen in teaching. You put the effort and work in and it's only several years down the track, if ever, that you will meet a former student who says, "Do you remember me? You taught me and I am so grateful to you." When I told people I cleaned houses, they would be surprised. "You *enjoy* doing that?" they would ask. And I do. I have met some wonderful, really interesting people in my cleaning work.'

'I also go to meetings and breakfasts organised by Home-Based Business Australia, and there I have met a wide cross-section of people and come into contact with businesses I never knew existed. My social interactions have actually widened. Teachers tend to mix with a narrow range of people, mainly other teachers.'

Having a business mentor can help improve self-esteem as well as business knowledge. Draftsman Peter Robertson still keeps in touch with his business mentor, whom he first met on the New Enterprise Incentive Scheme. 'Initially he inspired and educated me. Then, when I finished the course and started my own home-based business, we would have regular follow-up meetings at my home. He is still happy for me to ring him and that is very encouraging,' says Peter.

Managing your time

Working at home, you may find it all too easy to fall into a pattern of late morning starts and long lunches or, alternatively, hours spent on low-priority tasks. Have you heard the expression, 'Time is the coin of your life'? American poet Carl

Sandburg went on to say, 'It is the only coin you have, and only you can determine how it will be spent'. The American scientist–statesman Benjamin Franklin advised: 'Do not squander time, for that is the stuff life is made of.'

We all have the same amount of time in a day, so why is it that some achieve so much and others so little? Less sleep—is that how it's done?

Certainly, some workaholics do work day and night, but the answer is to *work smarter, not harder*. Author and advertising executive Bryce Courtenay believes it is immaterial whether you sleep four hours a night or fourteen. It's what you do with your waking hours that counts. He says most of us waste about four hours every day. Those who achieve most invariably manage their time well. They make the most of every hour.

Setting a routine

The first step in taking control of your time is to establish a routine or at least set core working hours. Decide what times of day and what hours you will work. Perhaps 9 to 5 will suit you; perhaps other commitments will not allow this. You may choose to work until early afternoon, collect the children from school, and continue your work once they are settled or asleep.

Are you a morning or evening person—a lark or a night owl? Now you can choose to work at the times when you are most productive—starting at dawn or in the late afternoon. The latter can be an ideal time to start business with overseas companies, since during the evening and night you will be in sync with their time zone. As a home worker, insomnia can bring great benefits!

Some people don't function well unless their hours are flexible. The hours they set are more like core working hours. 'If I wanted set working hours, I would have stayed in my last job,' says computer consultant Wesley Brown. 'I don't want to be regimented, starting and finishing work at the same time each day. For me, that defeats the whole purpose of working from home. I enjoy having flexible work hours.'

But whether your hours are rigid or flexible, once you've settled on a routine, stick to it! For home workers, this can take a lot of discipline. As dietitian and nutritionist Rosemary Stanton says, 'You can't be constantly leaving your work to duck out and clean the kitchen'. But if such self-control is not part of your nature, there is no need to fear. Psychologists say it takes three weeks to get into the habit of something new—21 days of rising at 6.30 a.m. for that early-morning walk before it becomes second nature and, hopefully, even a pleasure. It is the same with your work—it will take at least 21 days before most of us get into the swing of a routine and do it automatically. Perservere and your hours of work will become a pattern.

Setting your goals and priorities

Once your routine is in place, set yourself a weekly schedule and then a detailed daily timetable. What do you want to achieve this week? How will you divide the tasks up day by day? *Planning* is crucial if you work from home.

Andrew and Anne Cousins run a distribution business from home, operating with the Amway Corporation. They make daily lists prioritising their tasks. 'You need to ensure that you have something to achieve each day,' advises Andrew, 'otherwise it is all too easy to have cup after cup of tea.'

Andrew Matthews, too, makes a list of tasks he wants to accomplish each day, and places them in order of priority. *Prioritising* can be extremely helpful. You can classify your tasks in various ways, for example: a) Must do; b) Should do; c) Would like to do. Or a) Do immediately; b) Do next; c) Can wait. Sometimes it may be difficult to assign priorities. If this is the case, or if the tasks are of equal priority, place the *most challenging* ones at the top of your list. This may seem back to front. Far from it. Completing these tricky tasks *first* will encourage you and spur you on. Then, when you start to tire, only the quick and easy tasks remain. Remember—successful people also dislike doing certain tasks but the reason they are successful is precisely that they *do* them. It is not only by talent, or even because of it, that people become successful, but by application and perserverance. Successful people keep going long after others have given up.

It is important to write the tasks down rather than relying on memory. Re-reading the list prompts you to act on it and, by ticking the tasks off as you do them, you will gain a sense of accomplishment.

Be as specific as you can be with your daily goals. *What* size orders are you aiming for? *How* will you go about getting them? *When* will you need these orders to be placed?

Be realistic, too. Initially I found that I put far too much on my daily list. Not only did I overestimate the amount I could realistically do but I did not make allowance for any interruptions or unplanned changes to my schedule. One day, I had planned to finish writing a magazine article on abandoned dogs and then start preparing a workshop on writing biographies that I was to give in a few weeks' time. No sooner had I started on the article than the telephone rang. Actor Jack Thompson was available for interview that day and would ten o'clock be convenient? Since this was an interview I had been chasing for weeks and there was no way I could—or would—put it off, it unexpectedly became my top priority. As Thompson was filming in New Zealand at the time, the interview took place over the phone. Then I wrote up the story while our conversation was fresh in my mind. To accomplish that piece of work, though, I was forced to reschedule all my other assignments.

Such changes happen to everyone, so make allowances for them. And when setting your day's goals, don't overestimate what you can realistically achieve. Failure will only leave you disillusioned and despondent. Far better to write down a few tasks and accomplish them all, than to write down many and achieve hardly any of them. Indeed, I find writing down fewer tasks than I can feasibly complete motivates me to do more! *Remember to keep your goals realistic and attainable.*

When listing your daily goals, keep your eye fixed on your bigger aim. It is all too easy to get tied up in one aspect of the business or project to the detriment of everything else. Obviously the priorities you set will be affected by deadlines and payment, along with the amount of work involved. Look at what you are doing and why. It can be extremely helpful, too, to give yourself deadlines even when there are none.

David Kavenagh believes introducing short-term deadlines can get you really involved in a project. 'When I am working at home, I may tell myself that I'll write two pages of a report by 11 a.m. and then I'll go for a walk to the shops and treat myself to a cappuccino. By keeping this in mind, you can work without a lot of stress but with a lot of focus. There is a double bonus—this technique can help you get going and there is a bonus for staying with a task. You get the job done and a concrete reward for doing so. I don't necessarily do all these things all the time, but when I do, they work well.'

Short- and long-term goals

Have you heard the story about the mouse who set itself the task of eating an elephant? The determined rodent cut the massive pachyderm into small manageable pieces which it devoured daily until the elephant had completely disappeared. You, too, can accomplish large undertakings by breaking them down into small, controllable portions if you set short- and long-term goals.

If your long-term goal is to create a business with a million-dollar turnover, for example, how can you work toward this in short-term increments? You can set yourself the challenge of building up the business from scratch to having a $25,000 turnover in the first twelve months and then doubling this turnover each subsequent year. So you aim for a turnover of $50,000 by the end of year two, $100,000 by the end of year three and, in the first quarter of year six, you will have reached your long-term goal. So what are you waiting for?

Make sure your short- and long-term goals are compatible. It is really not feasible to have a short-term goal of spending most of your time with your family while having a long-term goal of becoming financially independent within five years. But then again, you could prove me wrong.

Beating procrastination

Set yourself unlimited time for a task and you are unlikely ever to complete it. Have you heard the saying 'If you want something done, ask a busy person'? If you ask someone who is *not* busy, he will tend to procrastinate, asking, 'What is the best way of doing this? When should I start? How long should I take? Is there any other way of doing this? Can I do a good job? What if it is not good enough?' Ask a busy person to do something and chances are he will start straight away, without stopping to think about it.

The phenomenon of procrastination is familiar to most of us. While the dictionary innocuously defines it as 'deferring or postponing action', those afflicted by procrastination know it can be an unwelcome and incapacitating ailment. As the Chinese proverb states: 'He who deliberates fully before taking a step will spend his entire life on one leg.'

You can read endless books and articles on procrastination. You can analyse *ad nauseam* the reasons for your procrastinating. Of course, in the time you have spent worrying about not starting the task, and asking yourself what is stopping you, you could have completed the task and saved yourself the anguish!

Have you ever said to yourself, 'I'll get down to work once I tidy my desk and make myself a cup of coffee'? While making the coffee, did you notice that the kitchen floor was a little grubby and think, 'I'll just quickly wipe it over'? Did you then glance out the window and wonder, 'Where did all those weeds spring from?' And did you find that before you knew it, you had a neat desk, a sparkling kitchen floor, a pristine garden—and a cold cup of coffee—and had still not done any work?

Stop stalling! Get on with it!

Interior designer Catherine Bugoss has put up a large sign in her office. It reads, 'DO IT NOW!' This is a good philosophy. Successful people do not find it any easier to work on certain tasks, they just *do* them instead of dithering, and move on.

It may also help you to try enjoying what you do rather than only doing what you enjoy. In a home-based business this can be especially pertinent, for you are responsible for, if not personally obliged to do, all the tasks associated with the business.

Here are a few tips on how to avoid procrastination:

- *Make sure your expectations are realistic.* If you plan to do too much, the prospect can become overwhelming and stop you from ever starting. Remember, *less is more.*
- *Make a list. Write* down what you aim to achieve.
- *Set deadlines.* Give yourself a time limit. Do you plan to

achieve these tasks today, this week, this month? Make sure your deadlines are realistic and attainable.
- *Become less perfect.* If you try to gather every scrap of information about snail farming, for example, you will become paralysed by the sheer quantity of data.
- *Start.* The Roman poet Horace said, 'He who has begun his task has half done it'.
- *Use your office only for work.* This will reinforce the idea that when you're there, you should be working.
- *Reward yourself.* Give yourself a small treat for completing your task.

We all tend to put things off, and the longer we do so, the harder it gets to start. Sometimes we stall, dither or hesitate because we feel the work has to be more than just right—it has to be perfect. Let go, relax, and you will find the task will flow much more easily. When really stuck, dismiss the saying 'If a thing's worth doing, it's worth doing well'. I heard a speaker at a seminar advise instead, 'If a thing's worth doing, it's worth doing badly and fixing up later'. If this applies in your situation, use it to get you moving. If you find you have a real block about a particular job, map it out roughly and then go back and fill in the gaps. Do the job somehow and then improve on it, rather than not starting on it at all.

At times, fear of failure can hold us back—as, strangely enough, can fear of success. Once again, the only way to tackle this problem is to leap in.

I was once commissioned to write an article on museums. Thinking it a tedious topic, I procrastinated, dealing with trivial and less urgent projects first, then just brooded over it! When my deadline loomed, I broke down the project into small, manageable portions and decided to spend a short time on it each day, so I would not become bored. As it happened, once I started I found museums to be a fascinating topic, and this turned out to be one of the most enjoyable pieces I have ever worked on.

Writer Libby Gleeson is all for 'doing the task right now'. 'You have to,' she maintains. 'I don't believe in sitting and waiting for the muse to strike. I do procrastinate, there's no question about that. But my tip is to get up and at it! If you're a writer, sit at your desk in your office with the door shut. Have a blank piece of paper in front of you and a pen or pencil in your hand. You will find that thoughts will come. I find I think much better with a pencil in my hand than without one.'

For those with computers, I recommend sitting in front of a blank screen, fingers poised on the keys. But first turn on the computer!

Evaluating yourself

Evaluate your performance. Are you on schedule, week by week and month by month? How are your finances—your income and your outgoings? If you find these are insufficient, go back one step to *prioritising.*

Once your business is established, you may find you are working long hours with little remuneration. Instead of continuing in this way, and perhaps even forcing yourself to work 'harder', look in detail at *what* you are doing. You may find that you are spending far too long on aspects of your work that do not pay well. As a journalist, for example, you might spend a week writing five articles that pay $100 each before tax, when you could spend a week on one article—albeit a far more complex one—that would pay $1,000.

Do you have the option of pursuing better-paid work or, alternatively, spending less time on the work that does not pay so well? Consider the 80:20 law: 80 per cent of your time may be spent on work that generates 20 per cent of your income, so why not focus on the 20 per cent that generates 80 per cent of your income? If 20 per cent of your customers give you work that accounts for 80 per cent of your income, concentrate on these bigger orders, save yourself time in work and earn more.

After you have been in business for a few months, ask yourself: Am I becoming more efficient? Set up your own 'time and motion' study. Analyse your day and then your week. How long are you spending on administration, on tasks not directly income-generating? In my case, this means things such as reading and responding to mail, searching out further work, sending out invoices and chasing them up, and bookkeeping. You may discover, to your horror, that this administration takes up a significant part of your day.

The well-known adage 'time is money' is not entirely correct. It is what you *do* with that time that is more accurate. '*Work* is money' would be fitting and preferable. By work, though, I mean income-generating work, not futile paper shuffling.

Look at how you spend your day and each evening and, like Andrew Matthews, ask yourself: 'What have I achieved today?' and 'How much income is that likely to generate?' Bear in mind that you are after *productivity* rather than just *activity.* Do not confuse action with accomplishments. Focus on your *results* rather than your *efforts.* 'Sometimes you might work for 100 hours in the week and you've done nothing. Sometimes you only put in a few hours but it's been extremely worthwhile,' says real estate advisor Jan Somers.

'Anne and I work a maximum of 30 hours a week,' says Andrew Cousins of his and his wife's involvement in multi-level marketing. This does not include time on the road, he adds: 'You would not count the time driving to and from your city office as work time.'

Organisation

This is another key element in the success of your business. But however unmethodical and disorganised you are, take heart. Like self-discipline, organising skills can be learned. Here are two golden rules:

> *Have a place for every item in your office and keep that item in its allocated place*; and
>
> *Handle each piece of paperwork once only.*

These two tips can save you hours of wasted time. If you know duplicates of customer invoices are kept in the top drawer of your filing cabinet, then you can quickly and easily locate Mr Dower's account instead of searching for ages through piles of papers scattered throughout your office. As for handling each piece of paper once only, you will halve your frustrations if you immediately replace Mr Dower's account in your files when you have finished with it. Toss it on your desk for filing later and you will increase your work and decrease your efficiency.

Develop a suitable and effective filing system. This may be easier said than done but, once in place and adhered to, it will make your life much easier. Writer Libby Gleeson has created a filing structure for herself. There is only one problem. 'Getting the papers from my desk to the files is where my system breaks down,' she laments. 'I tried taking Friday mornings off to remedy this but then I'd find myself meeting deadlines for Saturday morning talks.' Libby has a solution in mind. 'It requires a certain amount of willpower,' she says. 'I'm going to teach the children how to file and pay them for it!'

'I'm like a bowerbird, I don't like to throw anything out. The noticeboard in my office is covered with bits of paper, my in-tray is overflowing and I have stacks of stuff to file. Why do I keep it all—for posterity or future reference? I don't know,' laughs Libby.

Dealing with your clutter pile can take courage and stamina but it can also help to unclutter your life! When you eventually get round to sorting through a huge pile, it is bound to be a big task. You can avoid grief by following these tips:

- Block off some time in your diary, every week or every fortnight, to deal with the clutter pile. Stick to that time!
- Always place each item or piece of paper in its final destination. Do not handle a piece of paper more than once.
- Devise your own system whereby you tackle the clutter pile when it reaches a certain—manageable—size. That is, deal with it before your diary date, if need be.
- Every six to twelve months, block out a day to clear out your entire office and filing system.
- If you are an obsessive hoarder, learn to break this habit. Rip out and keep the articles you want rather than holding on to entire magazines. Instead of keeping newspapers or other disposable items 'in case I need them one day', dump them and make a note of where you can locate the information in a library, for example.

My cousin George in London once heard of an elderly woman who was exceptionally neat and tidy. When she died, the people clearing the house found she had been a methodical and compulsive collector, reluctant to throw anything out.

They came across a box labelled—and containing—'pieces of string too short to be used'.

Be warned—if it isn't curbed promptly and effectively, clutter can take over your life!

Home alone

This morning my laptop computer died on me. For some reason, it just refused to start. I felt like kicking it! Had I been in a busy office, I would merely have summoned a technician and worked on another computer while mine was being fixed. But I was alone and had no support. Well, not quite none.

I made a telephone call to my local computer shop and, unable to rectify the problem over the phone, Ashley Beeching, the proprietor, suggested I bring in my Powerbook. The battery was fully charged, my mains plug was perfect. He was at a loss. Replacing the battery, he pressed the switch. The computer booted up and proceeded to work perfectly!

I *could* have felt rather silly at that point, but I was overcome with relief rather than embarrassment. Having frequented the store in the past, I had got to know the staff, who also realised I worked from home. They would go out of their way to help me promptly, for they knew that without my computer I could not work. I, in turn, have recommended their professional, friendly and reliable service to others. So I may not have staff who can help me in the next room, but my support is just a telephone call away. Many are the times my problems have been solved that way.

Leaving the store that morning, smiling with relief, I remembered the experience of a friend of mine who will remain nameless. She, too, had found her laptop would not work one day. The familiar 'on' chord sounded when she turned it on, but the screen remained black. When she took her laptop in to a computer store, it was fixed in two seconds flat. The computer expert merely turned up the brightness control!

You can be your very own support person in such easy-to-solve emergencies if you take the trouble to familiarise yourself with your equipment, read articles or books and attend courses on it. When writer and desktop publisher Paula

Ruzek purchased her first computer and printer, she took time to thoroughly learn about the system and its capabilities. 'So began my love affair with computers. Now my whole business is based around computer technology', she enthuses.

Don't be one of those people who believe in reading the instruction book only when all else fails. Working on my last book, *A Different Light*, I sighed with satisfaction as I turned off my computer after a good afternoon's work. In my haste, I inadvertently clicked on 'no' rather than 'yes' when the question 'save changes before closing?' flashed up on the screen.

Several pages about Dr Tenshi Ayukai's work on the Great Barrier Reef were instantly wiped out! The words 'can't undo' came up on the screen as I frantically tried to retrieve my work. My first impulse was to scream. My second was to hurl the laptop across the room. I settled for a compromise and, while the material was still fresh in my mind, sat down again and re-typed it as best I could from memory. I even convinced myself that the second draft was an improvement! In that way, I refuted Paddy's Law. Murphy's Law claims, 'Whatever can go wrong will go wrong'. Paddy asserts, 'Murphy was an optimist'.

In any case, my experience with the lost pages taught me a valuable lesson. Had I saved each page as I had gone along, I would have lost—at most—a few lines of text. Had I printed out my day's work, I would still have it to copy from. Had I backed up my efforts on a computer disk, I would have been laughing rather than screaming. These days I overdo it a little and do all three. I'd rather be safe than sorry. And I have also attended a couple of computer courses, as well as studying the manual. I am convinced those lost pages are floating around somewhere in the system, still waiting to be found!

At home with your partner

Working with your partner at home is a potential minefield. Tempers can flare, angry words can be exchanged. I have even heard of a marriage breakdown in which working together was a contributing factor.

Some would never consider working with their partner, while others cannot contemplate another lifestyle.

If you do decide to work together, you need to be very clear about what your tasks are going to be, advises Jan Sutherland of Dial-A-Wife Cleaning Services. *Have clear and separate responsibilities and areas of expertise.* As well as preventing arguments and disagreements, this also helps you to keep up your self-esteem and confidence and increase efficiency. 'Once you clarify your tasks, you will ensure a better result,' says Jan. She did the initial market research for the business and set the charges. Now she deals with the public and trains the staff while husband Ross does the paperwork and teaches administrative skills to their employees. Jan sees herself as the 'people person, the risk-taker', while Ross is the 'keel or rudder that keeps me on an even balance'. They work well together, seeing their roles as complementary.

But it hasn't been easy. Jan believes it is important to ask a few questions when considering working together. Do you have the same goals in mind? Do these goals include making the business a success, supporting your financial future, being aware of giving a high-quality service? Does your partner complement you in your job?

Says Ross: 'There are difficulties in being with someone 24 hours a day, and we do have arguments occasionally. You need to *have time out from the business and away from each other.* It need not be a long time, just two hours or so. I go to the gym and play golf regularly.'

As for your relationship, Jan cautions, 'You need to be very careful to each treat the other as an employee of the company and not as a spouse. You can get blasé or complacent. Familiarity really does breed contempt and you need to avoid that.' Would you speak in the same tone and manner to a stranger, your employee, as you do to your partner? *Treat each other with respect.*

Andrew and Annie Cousins, who run a distribution business from home, find it a great advantage to be together. 'When I worked as a teacher, I would also be out coaching football for up to five nights a week. Annie and I would only have decent time together at weekends,' explains Andrew. 'I think working together is a fantastic idea, but do expect a few challenges if you are not used to being with one another so much and seeing one another in these business roles.' They, too, have different roles. Andrew shows people the concept of multi-level marketing and Annie offers support, particularly in the ordering and marketing of products, should their clients decide to join with them in business.

Andrew also advocates looking upon your partner as another employee of the company. 'Treat the other person as you yourself would like to be treated,' he says. 'That way, you can get the best out of one another.'

'Our attitude has been that we do everything 100:100. That way, if I don't do it, Annie will. So the job will get done,' says Andrew. 'If you do something 50:50 and someone does not do their part, then the whole business suffers.'

He believes that, far from damaging their relationship, working together has strengthened it. 'You are working together with your partner instead of someone else's,' he explains. 'The divorce rate today in Australia is 40 per cent, but the divorce rate in the IDA system (our support and training system) is less than 5 per cent.' Andrew says the IDA sets them on a course of self-improvement, with seminars, tapes and books. 'You learn how to work things out.'

Window cleaner Josh Zappone is certain that working together has made him and his wife Emma closer. 'Before, we would only see one another at night. Now we get to enjoy the time we have together. We take a full hour for lunch, instead of just a fifteen-minute break, and it becomes the highlight of our day—in as much as lunch can be a highlight! We'll make sandwiches or buy our lunch and go to the park.'

For Josh and Emma, it is early days yet. They have only been working together for a few months. Julie and Andrew Matthews have been co-directors of Andrew Matthews Productions for four years. 'Make the rules *before* you start!' says Julie. 'Talk business only from 8 or 9 a.m., whenever you start work. Otherwise you'll be lying in bed together, talking business before you even get up. You must also be disciplined enough to stop work at 6 or 7 p.m., whatever time you decide. Otherwise you will find that business dominates your whole life. Things will grate if that is all you talk about.'

Julie and Andrew have different interests—he plays tennis, often before breakfast, and she takes time out for walks on the beach. 'We were not always like this,' Julie admits. 'But we learned. Now we plan our holidays before the year starts, to make sure we take them. We mark the time off in the diary. We used to keep taking on work and saying we'd catch up with holidays the following year. We never did, and if you don't take regular breaks, you start getting niggly.' *Have time together to relax and forget about work.*

What about a slightly different situation—when you both work from home but in different businesses? 'I told Peter I married him for many reasons, but lunch was not one of them,' says dietitian and nutritionist Rosemary Stanton. 'I had to make it clear that I would not be getting lunch for him every day.'

Rosemary has been home-based for 28 years, but Peter joined her only a few years ago. This caused her some concern at first. 'I thought I would go mad but I didn't, and he thinks working together is wonderful. I did initially resent having him there, as I work very long hours and like to have a break at lunchtime and read the paper. I thought I would no longer be able to do that but in fact it's worked out really well. When I'm not here, he will answer the telephone and take messages and I will do the same for him,' says Rosemary.

'We have separate offices, and it is important for the offices to be far enough away so that you cannot hear one another on the phone. And you do not have to explain who is ringing. You need to maintain a degree of integrity. It is essential to have separate telephone and fax lines.'

After 23 books and almost 3,000 newspaper and magazine articles, Rosemary has finally admitted to herself that she finds switching off from work a problem. 'But I'm getting better,' she says. 'I have a great capacity for work and always have gone back to it after dinner, simply because it is so accessible. Now I have taken up gardening, and I've developed a real passion for it.'

Valerie Britton Wilson started work as a home-based qualitative researcher in the 1970s, when the concept was still new in Australia. 'I had spent some time working in this way in London and thought it was terrific. Once back in Melbourne, I struck up an arrangement with my previous employer.' She has continued in this way ever since, with breaks when raising her children and studying. Now she's been joined by her husband, John, whom she describes as a 'lapsed lawyer who is now an investor and fiction writer'.

'At first I found it quite hard because this was not just my domestic territory but also my work territory. But once we had worked things out, it was better,' she says. 'We both work best in the mornings, we put our heads down and get on with it. We do not interrupt one another in the first hour of work, when we are most productive. We meet for a cup of coffee at 10 o'clock and for lunch once or twice a week, circumstances permitting. Today was a fairly typical day. I have a sick child at home, I've done five loads of washing and I did the supermarket shopping in the lunch hour.'

Computer consultant Wesley Brown found home-based work presented problems at the outset. 'If my wife, Tina, wants the car and a client rings, then that takes priority. In the beginning that was a hassle and caused friction,' he says, 'but that's where the money comes from—clients.' Tina sees having Wesley at home as an advantage rather than a disadvantage. 'The children love it, too, but once a week we get a babysitter and go out for a meal together, just the two of us.'

At home with children

Wesley Brown is fortunate. He can concentrate totally on his work. 'He can switch off from the children and work on his computer, not even knowing they're there,' says Tina. That's all well and good if there is another carer in the house, but if you are responsible for the children or if you and your partner are both working at home, things can be a little tougher.

It's important, as early as possible, to explain your work situation and guidelines to your children in language they can understand. Draftsman Peter Robertson has explained to his nine-year-old daughter Leah that although Daddy is now always at home, he cannot devote all his time to her. 'When she comes home from school, she will ask, "Can you do this?" and I'll say, "No, I'm working." She understands now and will amuse herself until I have finished.'

When it comes to toddlers, Libby Gleeson has it all worked out. 'You are kidding yourself if you think you can run a business from home alongside small children, unless you can run that business on two hours' work a day. What would you do if you had to go out to work? You would find childcare outside the house or get someone to come in.' Libby picked the former option. When she worked part-time she would take her youngest child to childcare two or three days a week. 'I almost never work when the three children are at home,' she says, 'only if there are deadlines.'

Qualitative researcher Valerie Britton Wilson has found she has to be strict with her three youngsters. 'They put more demands on you when they know you are home,' she admits. 'The children are more likely to ring and ask me to bring in the hockey stick they left at home. They wouldn't do that if I was in an office. It is frustrating but it would be more so if I was working elsewhere. Then I would have to lose a day's work if a child was ill. This is much better. At least I can do some work if they are ill.'

Some years ago, Valerie went to a school talk 'where a family very much like ours spoke about relationships. Both parents worked from home and there were three children. The children said the usual things about the advantages of their parents being home but they did not see it as all good. They were troubled by the fact that there was no clear dividing line between work and play time with the parents. They sometimes felt bad for interrupting their parents, and their parents' attention was often divided. The kids said they did not have enough structured leisure time with their parents because of that.' Like Libby, Valerie does not even try to work when the children are home and awake. 'I drop everything between 3 and 8 p.m. and I sometimes go back to it after dinner.'

Motivation

Some mornings Jan Sutherland, of Dial-A-Wife, would cry from exhaustion, not wanting to work, bemoaning the fact that she had no holiday or sick pay and that she had to carry on regardless. How did she—and how can you—find the motivation to continue?

We all—even the most successful—have days when we can't be bothered to work. It may all seem too difficult. Business has not been going well recently, so why go on? You have run out of steam, the effort is all too much. Besides, it's a beautiful day outside, so why not take the day off and relax? At times like this, Jan asks herself, '*Why* am I doing this?' Her reply: 'I would rather be working for myself than having to answer to another person. I also have the freedom to express myself in my own business. I have the challenge of discovering entrepreneurial skills. And apart from all of that—who else is going to feed our family?'

Having come to that conclusion, Jan gets herself going by getting out of bed, having a shower and dressing to start her day.

Many books have been written on motivation and many people, like Jan, find them useful. One terrific book is *The Seven Habits of Highly Effective People*, by Stephen R. Covey, Melbourne, Victoria, Business Library, 1990.

Some fortunate individuals have no difficulty with drive. 'I'm a very motivated person,' says Adelaide dress designer Margaret Moore. 'I'm up by 6 and have put in half a day's work by 9 o'clock. I've always worked on the principle that life is too short, so I don't want to waste a minute.'

In addition to her determined disposition, Margaret's motivation comes from *competition.* 'When I started out as a dress designer in the United Kingdom, I soon discovered that it was not enough for my garments to be just average. They had to be much better than average or they would not sell. And if they did not sell, I would no longer have a job.' Not only did this fact spur Margaret on but it also gave her constant motivation for improvement.

Talking with other home-based business owners can be a helpful way of motivating yourself. Discussing your problems with others in the same area can provide you with solutions. Chances are, they have also been through this. Remember, however hard it gets, even in your darkest moments, you are *not* alone. There is always help and support available, whether it be from other colleagues or home-based associations.

By establishing your own professional network, you can exchange ideas and trade clients. Such regular social contact can boost flagging morale while keeping you in touch with the latest business developments. More structured organisations, such as Home-Based Business Australia, are also recommended in this regard.

Jan Sutherland says, 'It can be really hard when you work alone keeping your business afloat. Home-Based Business Australia meetings are a good place to network and to learn new ideas you can implement in your business. I might feel disgruntled about something and another member might have a good idea on how to deal with it.' Jan is also a member of the Women's Business Network. 'I attend breakfasts and listen to speakers. I am inspired by successful people such as Ita Buttrose and Kerry Packer.' She also reads books and listens to tapes.

One television designer found that, when reading scripts at home for which he had to create sets, he would invariably fall asleep. He discovered that, curiously, in the noisy and stimulating atmosphere of the local pub, with a single beer to last all evening, he could concentrate much better. It worked for him!

It is important to get out of the house from time to time. Otherwise your work environment can become oppressive. 'I have commitments to committees,' says writer Libby Gleeson. 'I go to meetings of the Sydney Writers' Festival and Community Arts Marrickville. I am also involved in my children's schools.' Julie Matthews believes in the value of taking an afternoon or day off, out of the house and away from your partner. 'Otherwise you would not have anything new to talk about,' she says.

Looking after yourself

Security

The fact that you are on your home premises for much of your time can provide additional security for your property and contents. But make sure your house has adequate security measures in place for when you are out. These can include window bars or locks, a burglar alarm or a guard dog. Make sure your insurance policy is valid and covers all office equipment. Be thoughtful when recording the message for your telephone answering machine. 'I'm out at the moment' can serve as a welcome invitation to a burglar. 'I (or we) are unavailable at present' is far more sensible. If you do not want callers to know you live alone, you may prefer 'we'. You might also restrict your contact hours with clients, not seeing them at home after dark and making sure someone else is in the house with you when clients call. Alternatively, you could visit them.

Diet and exercise

You may find cooking a bore, a hassle or too time-consuming. Constantly eating out or buying takeaway food can play havoc with both your stomach and your wallet. Try always to have some nutritious, tasty food on hand, or learn some easy-to-prepare recipes. Cooking can help you unwind and thus aid your mental well-being. Just three sessions of 30 minutes a week doing a sport or activity you enjoy can keep your body fit and healthy. I find I can concentrate far better at my work after a game of tennis and that swimming helps clear my mind.

Overwork, sickness and holidays

Who would have thought you would be in the position of worrying about *over*working? But when you work for yourself, overwork is a distinct possibility. Beware of burn-out and aim to avoid it by taking regular breaks and short holidays. 'Holidays? What are holidays?' asks Jenny Church of Your Type Secretarial Services. 'I do manage a clear week over Christmas, but I can't leave my business unattended for too long. I had to use temporary staff when I had the flu but luckily I don't get sick often.'

Holidays can be a difficulty for small-business owners. Yet it is vital to make time for them. Don't learn the hard way, by putting holidays off and off until you become thoroughly exhausted or ill.

Speaking of which, does your insurance policy cover you for sickness and accidents? Can you make an arrangement with a similar business to cover for you when you are ill or absent?

Optimism

'To accomplish great things, we must not only act, but also dream, not only plan, but also believe,' I once read on a poster. Optimism is fundamental. Author Bryce Courtenay says of success, 'I don't think it is a question of time or any special ability. I think it's a question of understanding, having confidence that you can do it'. And you *can* do it. You know you can! The door to success is, after all, labelled 'Push'.

REVIEW

Time management

Plan Prioritise Evaluate
Set yourself a weekly schedule and a daily timetable.

Organisation

- Develop a suitable and effective filing system and stick to it.
- Handle each piece of paperwork once only.
- Have a place for every item in your office and keep that item in its allotted place.

Averting procrastination

- Make sure your expectations are realistic.
- Make a list, but keep your goals attainable—remember less is more.
- Set deadlines and keep them.
- Use your office for work only.
- Reward yourself for completing the task.
- Become less perfect.

Separating work life from family life

- If possible, have a separate physical space put aside for your office. This will give you privacy, productivity and peace of mind.
- Have set core working hours and set aside time for relaxation.

- Respect your partner and family.

Security

- Have adequate security measures—window locks or bars, burglar alarm, guard dog.
- Make sure your insurance policy is valid and covers all office equipment.
- Have an appropriate message on your answering machine—'we are unavailable at present'.
- Restrict contact hours with clients or avoid seeing them at home.

Coping with children

- Explain to the children, in language appropriate to their age, that you now work from home.
- Set guidelines for the children.
- Let the children know at what times you are not to be interrupted, except in case of emergency.
- Learn to be patient and flexible. Expect and deal with extra demands placed on you by children.
- Never attempt to run a home-based business alongside small children. Get childcare.
- Set aside play time for your children.

Handling friends and neighbours

- Make it clear that you are *working* from home.
- Answer the telephone with your business name.
- Tell friends and neighbours that you will speak to them after work.
- Put the answering machine on at times when you do not want to be disturbed.

Dealing with other distractions

- Develop self-discipline.
- Learn to say no.
- Choose not to see housework during work hours.
- Share chores with your partner.
- Hire a cleaner.

Decide to do, in your work day, only what you would do if you were working away from home.

Social isolation

Avoid social isolation by:

- keeping up your friendships;
- having lunches occasionally and coffees frequently with friends; and
- using the telephone, e-mail and letters to keep in touch.

Counteract professional isolation by:

- joining professional bodies and organisations;
- subscribing to newsletters and journals; and
- initiating regular meetings with work colleagues.

Overcome loss of social status and self-esteem by:

- joining a home-based organisation; and/or
- finding a business mentor.

Motivation

Beat lack of motivation by:

- reminding yourself of the reasons you have chosen to work from home;
- remembering the advantages of working from home;
- taking action;
- planning your strategy;
- setting yourself goals and doing the most challenging ones first;
- networking; and
- getting out of the house regularly.

Stay motivated with:

- a balanced and nutritious diet; and
- regular exercise—30 minutes three times a week.

Overwork, sickness and holidays

- Avoid overwork and sickness by taking regular breaks in your work day.

- Have contingency plans for illness — other colleagues to take over your work and insurance to cover your salary.
- Take holidays. Short regular vacations can be more effective than one long one. There may be appropriate times in the year for holidays, when work is slower.

Remember you are the most important asset of your business—take good care of that valuable asset.

A HOME FROM HOME

Rosemary Stanton's commitment to working at home is reflected in the fact that she has not one but *two* home offices. Australia's leading nutritionist uses one office—in rural New South Wales, where there is peace and quiet—for writing her books and articles, and her Sydney office for seeing clients.

Rosemary has been working from home, as a dietitian and nutritionist, for 28 years. 'When I started, I had a separate entrance to the study from which I worked but people still knocked at the front door! So I built a separate building altogether. I felt I needed to be separate from the house as I had four small children. I ran a private practice from there. When the children came home from school, they could buzz me on the intercom and I had the flexibility to go and have afternoon tea with them. I was at home for ten years before having the separate building.'

Rosemary and her husband Peter now live in the country. In the last five years he too has started working from home, writing computer programs. 'I needed to see private patients, so I bought a terrace house in Sydney,' Rosemary says. 'The consulting room is on the ground floor and I can live upstairs. I'm in town two or three days a week and one of my daughters lives there permanently. I am so wedded to the home-office concept that I did not rent an office. Instead I found this location suitable for professional use at Woollahra. I can officially work from there. I looked for a while, avoiding units and apartments. I was searching for a house with a waiting room and a consulting room at the front and a separate hallway. This area could be divorced from the rest of the house. Otherwise you would be spending your entire life keeping the house tidy. It would not be professional to have washing hanging off the back of kitchen chairs. Without such a separation, you would feel your house was constantly on show.'

For the remainder of her week, Rosemary enjoys living in the country. She and Peter have offices at opposite ends of the house, with an intercom connecting them. They usually meet for morning tea and lunch. 'He works for an employer in the UK, so he does not need a city office,' Rosemary explains.

In addition to her other work, Rosemary regularly gives radio, newspaper, magazine and television interviews. She is a regular presenter on *Burke's Backyard*. 'Having both a country kitchen and a city kitchen is an advantage,' she says. 'It is beneficial having two different locations for filming. Working from home gave me flexibility for the children when they were young. I could go to Easter bonnet parades and then work late at night. I like having plants outside my window and deciding when I want to do something. Another reason, maybe a strange one, to why I work from home, is that I can't stand being in airconditioned offices. I like open windows, not stuffy offices, and while I do have an airconditioner now, at least *I* have the choice of turning it on or off. I tend to work long hours. There is more tendency to do that from home, otherwise you would have to drive into the office. But I'm getting better at curbing it. I'm developing a passion for gardening.'

INTERNATIONAL LIVES

Montgomery Omodei thought no one would employ him at the age of 47, so he decided to go into business for himself. 'I had been an executive director of large companies and at my age I was not easily employable. Organisations have cleared out those 40 and above from management positions. I did not want to go on social security. I had experience, contacts and abilities, so I decided to work on my own, from home,' he says.

Five years on, Montgomery works from his Gold Coast base as an international business advisor and lobbyist. He represents overseas corporations in the areas of mining and petroleum and acts as a trader's representative for base metal. All his clients are based offshore. He introduces them to the Australian business markets and helps them to achieve their goals. The companies for which he works may have assets of billions of dollars—working from home in his case is certainly not small-time!

Having his business integrated with home life enables Montgomery to run a 24-hour, seven-day-a-week enterprise should he choose to do so. 'I may work 25 days one month and five days the next,' he explains. 'My wife Janet's support role in my business has been vital to its success. She has been dedicated, hard-working and understanding in creating a balance between business and our private lives. As well as everything else, you have to be good friends.' One of the main advantages of a home base for him is the flexibility. Communicating by telephone, e-mail, the Internet or fax machine, he can be available at all times—from early evening to make contact with Europe and from midnight on for the US. 'International dealings come in at different times, but you can deal with them,' says Montgomery. 'I see myself just as a man who went out on his own and found he could earn a good living. I started my business in hard times. And to keep a small business running over six years, you need good ideas to keep going.'

Three company directors located in three different states? It sounds incredible but it works well. Roger Fountain, Steve Reutens and Ray Green head Seedex Pty Ltd, operating from their homes in Byron Bay, Brisbane and Geelong respectively. They started by specialising in the oilseed market, 'doing what the big crushers can't do,' explains Steve. 'We deal with a niche-type market, a lower volume but higher margins, while large companies look at big volumes.' Seedex not only crushes but trades oilseed.

'We are big in the organic market, which is booming in Europe and the US and just taking off in Japan.'

Between them, the three men have 80 years of experience. They started Seedex in 1990 and this limited liability company is now the largest supplier of organic vegetable oils worldwide. 'We've done well through a combination of technology and expertise,' Roger says. He handles the trading side of the company, frequently travelling overseas, while Steve is the financial controller and Ray works in the field, making contact with seed growers. Mobile telephones have made communication between the three of them easier and they also have regular three-way meetings via conference calls.

Roger moved to Byron Bay from Sydney, where he was working as a commodity trader. 'I was fed up with the traffic and pollution and spending more than two hours a day travelling to and from Parramatta,' he says. 'I'd had enough of the city.' For eight years, he, wife Nancy and their two children have lived in a large red-cedar house with an orchard, set on 47 acres. 'It is clean, healthy living here at Byron Bay—a great climate, green paddocks and no noisy neighbours. My hours are flexible and I don't have to sit in an office under fluorescent lighting all day. And if nothing's doing late afternoon, I can switch on my answering machine and go surfing.'

With the aid of a computer and modem, Roger can check the global markets daily and immediately respond to the news that the price of canola seed has changed in France or that a sunflower crop has failed in Argentina. 'We can be far more productive than other Australian companies,' says Roger. 'We can respond to international seed buyers by fax within a few minutes when other companies are closed. And, with my digital phone, I can be contacted just about anywhere in the world.' When he's on the road, Roger's office is in his briefcase. This contains his portable computer and modem.

In 1997, Steve swapped one rural environment for another, relocating to New South Wales when the company started its own specialist crushing plant in western Sydney.

'The plant is set on 1,000 acres of land and I am looking out of my office window at cattle, horses and sheep.'

'I also have a home office and all my calls and faxes can be diverted there,' says Steve, who lives in Australia's oldest private residence, Claremont Cottage at Windsor.

Steve is thinking of leaving his home office altogether. 'It was great initially but now I find it interrupts family life. Whenever the telephone rings or a fax comes through, you feel you have to deal with it. Not to do so would be self-defeating. My wife might want to stay at home at weekends but I want to go to town, as I've been at home all the time. To keep your family life sane, I think you have to work elsewhere.'

Home-based or not, the three men make a good team and have been highly successful *because* of their age and experience rather than despite it.

9

THE FUTURE

Home-based business is neither an industry nor a market but a culture, according to Pamela LaPersonne of *HomeBiz* magazine. 'It is a lifestyle option and one that is on the increase,' she says. 'People often ask me what are the most common home based industries. You can't pin it down to twenty or even thirty areas, it goes right across the board. What surprises me is how many professionals and manufacturers are now working out ways of operating from home. People want choices about when and how they work. They find the bonuses are being their own boss, being rewarded for their own efforts and having no ceiling on the income they make.'

Home-based business is a trend that is growing rapidly and one that is here to stay, although it may alter slightly in form, says Professor Jack Wood, Director of the MBA Program, Monash Mount Eliza Business School, Monash University. Because 'advances in technology are so sophisticated, so rapid and so smart that it is too expensive to keep up with them in a home office,' he foresees a levelling out in the number of home offices and a corresponding growth in high-tech satellite offices. 'People will commute to their nearest satellite office,' he says. 'This is already taking place aound Los Angeles and is starting to happen around Tokyo.' Resort offices have also been created, offering a trade-off between work and leisure. 'A cluster of resort offices now exists around Mount Fuji. They are fully equipped with the latest technology, including videoconferencing facilities,' says Professor Wood. 'They present a less work-oriented environment, where Japanese businessmen can ski during the day in winter, play golf during summer, and work in the evenings. The aim is to stop burn-out from overwork.'

Bob Ansett believes that Australia follows the US experience, albeit five years later. 'When I was recently in the United States, I was impressed to discover that a total of 33 million people now work from home,' he says. 'That is 15 per cent of the workforce.' Of this total, 25 million work from home for themselves while 8 million work at home for a company based elsewhere. 'The trend over there is to move away from the dense populations of the east and west coasts to the Rocky Mountain states, where the air and water are clear and the population low.

'Working from home will become increasingly significant in Australia, with the quality-of-life factor having some bearing on this decision,' says Ansett, who is one of the estimated 400,000 Australians (4 to 5 per cent of the workforce) who work at home. He moved his marketing business to Noosa, Queensland, fifteen months ago purely for the lifestyle, having decided that 'I can work as easily from here as from Melbourne or Sydney. My neighbours in Noosa are Americans who have chosen to live here and work in the US. He is a share trader, accessing US stock exchanges by computer modem, and she is a trial lawyer who flies back regularly to the US for work. This is an extreme example of work having no boundaries. The globe is becoming ever smaller.'

Meantime, our houses may be growing larger. Bill Hamill, former chief executive of Australia's largest real estate group, First National Real Estate, considers our country to be in the midst of a home-based-business revolution. First National's research has found that more than 700,000 households, 12 per cent of the total, have the capacity to be involved in home-based business. In Sydney, 15 per cent of home buyers purchase a house with a home office; in Hobart the corresponding figure is 6 per cent. 'Drive down the streets in suburbs such as South Melbourne, and you will see numerous signs advertising printing or consultancy services, interspersed between the terrace houses.'

Local governments and councils have begun approving residential/commercial zoning, and 'commercial apartments' are springing up in clusters. A group of townhouses in central Adelaide uses this living and working potential as its main selling point. Areas have been put aside for similar developments in Queensland, and the New South Wales Blue Mountains and central coast.

While a home office may not presently necessarily increase the value of your home, it can increase your chances of later selling the house, says Hamill. 'Having a home office opens up the property to a bigger audience. Those wanting to work from home will certainly look on this as a more favourable investment.'

As a result of the home-business trend, new industries are developing. 'Furniture is now being made to cater for the home office,' Hamill says. He describes a desk housing a computer which, with the press of a button and the flick of a lever, converts into an antique-style desk. 'There are filing cabinets that disappear in the evening and transform into wine racks and a wine bar! Furniture has been evolved that is totally functional during the day for an office set-up and then closes up at night for a home look.'

'In the future, people are going to see working from home as a viable option,' agrees Margaret Seedsman, National Executive Director of Home-Based Business Australia. 'People will no longer be content to stay in jobs they hate. They will see that there are alternatives, that they can instead do work that they enjoy.

'There are more single-parent families these days and many in this situation choose to work from home,' she says. 'I know of one man who has custody of his children every other week. He decided to work from home because of this. He bought a larger property and is there and available when the children return from school. For him, working from home means making the most of his time with his children. For others, the elimination of travel time is a big consideration. Cutting down on commuting reduces stress for the individual, and noise and pollution for the community.'

Margaret also believes that governments are giving those working from home greater recognition. 'Governments and councils are taking more and more interest. I'm presently co-operating with local government to help form networks.'

Home-Based Business Australia itself, founded in Melbourne in 1992, is growing rapidly. 'I'm getting more and more calls and we can't keep up with them,' says Margaret. A hotline has now been set up to keep up with the demand. There are currently over 5,000 members on the database and branches have been formed in New South Wales, Queensland and the Australian Capital Territory.

New opportunities are being created for home-based workers all the time.

Most of these are the direct result of advances in information and communications technology. Would you like to work from home for a company as a travel consultant or receptionist? You can work short shifts, perhaps just a couple of hours, picking up extra work but avoiding long commutes. How does becoming a 'content editor' for a CD-ROM appeal? Paul Holland is general manager of ICE T Multimedia, which finances, develops and publishes multimedia titles for the world market, as well as developing a range of on-line solutions for corporate, government and general markets. With seventeen full-time staff in its Queensland and Victorian offices, the company hires thirty or more contractors for periods of days, weeks and even months.

'These contract workers, who happen to be home-based, are graphic designers, animators, computer programmers and writers,' explains Paul. 'The latter may be script writers or content editors, who take the raw content, written by a technical person, and re-write it for a visual medium.

'The advantage to us of using people outside the organisation is that we don't get stale,' says Paul. 'Using in-house staff all the time, you can easily fall into an in-house style. We are constantly injecting fresh blood, new input, to avoid this. The challenge for people like myself is to manage these workers and to ensure the quality of the product. The flexible use of outworkers means that we do not require an enormous infrastructure. When you have employees, you need to provide technology for them and management infrastructure,' says Paul. 'It can seem expensive to hire people from outside, but there are lots of hidden costs associated with permanent staff. With contract or outworkers, you do not have to become big yourself in a corporate sense.'

Some industries depend on home-based workers. First National Real Estate has regional managers who work from home. 'The field force has done so for a number of years,' says Bill Hamill. 'There is no longer any real need to drive in from the suburbs into the office. Using new technology, workers can access the office from home.'

Ann Moffat, of Technology Solutions, says the biggest shift to using home-based workers is in the tertiary sector—government, banks, insurance companies and so on. 'These account for 75 per cent of all jobs in Australia and I think 80 per cent of these jobs could be done from home. Only about half of the people in these jobs, however, will decide they want to work from home.'

Hot desking

Working from home has given rise to new ways of working in offices. Try telling someone you are going to be hot desking today, and check out the reaction. The reality may not be *quite* as exciting as they imagine. It simply means sharing an office space with several others. A company whose employees do not need the full-time use of their office—because they work from their home or from their car—may decide to have fewer desks than people.

Management consulting firm Andersen Consulting has 80 managers sharing twelve offices and over 200 consultants sharing 30 workstations, resulting in huge cost savings. 'We have saved $1.5 million in the fit-out costs for additional offices,' says Derek Young, managing partner of Andersen Consulting in Melbourne, 'plus hundreds of thousands of dollars in rent for additional space.' For Andersen's, cost-cutting was a main consideration, but staff reaction was assessed before hot desking was implemented. Employees now book a 'Just in Time office' in advance, for the day or two a week that they may need it. They spend the rest of their working time away from the main office.

Hot desking requires an efficient central storage system and individual lockers for personal belongings and working files. A sophisticated telephone system which can divert incoming calls to the appropriate office is also needed. The Sydney office of Andersen Consulting takes this concept one step further, with 'hotelling'. Managers are able to book offices and other facilities—for example, meeting rooms—ahead of time, electronically via their computer notebooks.

Ann Moffat is managing director of Technology Solutions, a virtual company based in Sydney. 'I have 200 computer professionals at my disposal. They work from home whenever they can, come together when needed and are paid only when they work.' Ann, who had a similar set-up, with 400 staff members, in the United Kingdom, sees hot desking as just another way of organising an office environment. 'There is no need for a desk full-time. IBM in America use hot desking—you'll go in for work in the morning and be allocated a desk, say Desk 3 on Aisle 23. In big consultancy firms in the US you can call to book a desk and the concierge will prepare one for you. Some concierges go so far as to have Polaroid photos of your desk set-up so they can put it together in exactly the same way you left it!'

Ann says telecommuting is widely used by large companies. 'AMP salesmen, for example, all work from home and always have done so. They may go to the local sales office once a week and to the head office regularly.'

Tele-jargon

Today SOHO is no longer a district of London, teleguerillas are not necessarily aggressive and you may have a virtual office when working from home.

The fastest-growing type of workplace in Australia is the Small Office Home Office, otherwise known as SOHO. This is manned by a new breed of workers—teleguerillas, who work from home on an irregular basis, not having a formal agreement with their employer. And do you have a virtual office? 'Well, yes,' you might say, 'it's *almost* a proper office.

Once I remove the children's toys and build some bookshelves . . .' No, no, no. A virtual office is one that disappears when you do. 'When you go,' says Professor Jack Wood, 'someone else uses—or hot desks—it. This can also be called "hotelling" or "motelling".'

Another variation on the virtual office is the mobile office, consisting of a laptop computer, a modem and a mobile phone in a briefcase.

Savings

Whereas the 1980s may have been seen as a time of excesses, the 1990s are all about savings—in costs and space. 'Today's brief calls for flexibility and value for money,' says Peter Geyer of Geyer Design. 'We have a no-frills approach.' Having fitted out BHP's head office in Melbourne and the John Fairfax offices at Darling Park in Sydney, as well as the offices of Andersen Worldwide in Melbourne, Peter aims for a look that is not ostentatious but rather lean and mean. 'These companies recognise their people are out of the office for the majority of the time and so are planning accordingly,' he explains. 'One company manager, wanting a fit-out for his premises, walked through all the offices one weekday, capturing on video the activity at 10 a.m. and 3 p.m.,' says Geyer. 'When he showed the video to his partners, they could not believe it had been taken during office hours. They were convinced he had come in on a Saturday, as the offices were so desolate.' The manager did not have to work hard to convince his partners about the savings they could make by optimising the use of office space!

'You do save a lot of money but designing more shared work areas also encourages teaming,' says Geyer. 'It is good for consultants who have been out on the road all week to come back to the office and interact with others. We are concentrating far more on the group these days. Individual space is smaller than it used to be.'

And office management styles are changing, becoming less hierarchical. When Geyer Design was approached to refit the offices of Bankers Trust in Sydney, the company had 139 offices for 1,100 people. After the new fit-out there were 30 offices capable of accommodating 1,800 people. 'It was important that this company already had a culture that would enable this to happen,' says Geyer. 'Other companies may want the same set-up but they are struggling—their culture gets in the way, the company is too hierarchical, the office is seen as a status symbol. Rewards have to be given in other ways—perhaps a financial bonus rather than a big office in the corner.'

Leading the way

Australia may be leading the way, not so much in numbers but in other respects, for home-based workers. 'As far as I am aware, Australia is the first country in the world to have a home-based award for public sector workers,' says Gerardine McNamara, national industrial officer with the Community and Public Sector Union. This Commonwealth interim award came into effect on 14 February 1994, has since been reviewed and continues unamended.

'We could see what would arise in the future with the advances in technology,' says McNamara, 'and we wanted to take the initiative rather than react to what was going to happen.' Of the 100,000 public servants technically eligible to be home-based, only 150 had applied to do so by September 1995. Eighty-five of these had been approved and 65 rejected.

'It has not taken off in a big way,' McNamara admits. 'There is still a long way to go.' She says those who have received approval to work from home part-time come primarily from middle rather than senior or lower levels. 'They are in positions where they can work independently, not needing to be under close supervision and not participating in teamwork.'

The Senate Economics References Committee has looked closely into the future of telecommunications. Their November 1995 publication, *Connecting you Now—Telecommunications Developments Towards the Year 2000*, Parliament of the Commonwealth of Australia, Senate Printing Unit, Parliament House, Canberra, recommends that a large feasibility study be undertaken into outsourcing for government data-input requirements; that telecentres be allocated sufficient funding; that the Commonwealth Department of Employment, Education and Training trial a jobs brokerage scheme for teleworking;

and that the government be open to the possibilities of teleworking and telecommuting.

Resources

One of the challenges of working from home is equipping yourself with the appropriate technology. In certain careers, this can prove costly. 'Our graphic designers and computer programmers need a substantial home set-up,' says Paui Holland of ICE T Multimedia. 'The hardware and software can cost at least $10,000 to $20,000. You *can* manage on a shoestring for a while, but eventually the lack of technology will become an impediment.'

But there are other ways to get access to computer technology. There are 118 telecottages located in rural and remote areas throughout Australia (though not the Northern Territory) which are used by up to 10,000 people.

A telecottage or telecentre is a community access point for the delivery of services in enterprise development, education and training. Such centres contain state-of-the-art technology, including computers, modems, scanners, fax machines, photocopiers and colour printers. They also have Internet facilities. Their users are diverse, ranging from restaurant owners wishing to print menus to students typing out course assignments and home-based businesses sending faxes interstate or overseas. Prices are reasonable and using the facilities is certainly much cheaper than purchasing the equipment for yourself.

The first telecottage came into being in Walcha, NSW, in 1992. Since then, the federal Department of Primary Industries and Energy has funded 43 projects, the Western Australian government has funded 34, and service clubs and local councils have funded 4. Their locations range from Cygnet, Tasmania to Tumby Bay, South Australia.

Tips from the top

'People say you need to be disciplined when working from home,' says Pamela LaPersonne of *HomeBiz* magazine. 'I'd say it is not so much being *disciplined* as being *methodical.* You need to have a method of getting the work done by the time it has to be done.'

Pamela also believes in being able to say no. 'This is so much more important than when you are in an outside office. Friends, family and neighbours often ask you to do things for them. They think you are not working when you are at home. It all comes back to control—being in total control of what you do, when you do it, and how you do it.'

Pamela's third point is to take your business finances very seriously. 'This is where people tend to fall down or get stuck. The area of finances often tends to get overlooked. But you need to keep marketing, keep selling and keep the business growing.'

Putting a spoke in the works

Ann Moffat of Technology Solutions believes the signs of a good home-based worker are not a tidy desk or excellent time management but first-rate communication and negotiating skills. 'Make sure you are always saying what you mean—clearly *and* effectively,' she advises. 'You may think you are saying something clearly, but it's not much use if the other person does not respond.

'Be able to negotiate, too. People tell me, "I thought my husband would be available, working at home, but he works every evening" or "My wife gets angry if I don't bring the washing in when it rains. I'm working, I don't notice it is raining. Besides, if we were both out at work, the washing would get wet anyway. So what's the difference?" These couples need negotiating skills. They need to work out these issues for themselves.'

As for your appearance, Moffat has some interesting views. 'I really think working from home is an attitude of mind and of lifestyle. You can't make all people do the same thing, there are all sorts of ways to operate. Personally, I don't care whether your hair is blue, green or brindle and whether you work in a bathrobe. I am not concerned whether your desk is a pigsty but about what you produce. Your client looks at the quality, the price and the timeliness of your work. It is not *how* you work but what you *produce* that counts.' She says, 'The biggest shift to using home-based workers is in the tertiary sector—government, banks, insurance companies and so on. These account for 75 per cent of all jobs in Australia and, I think, 80 per cent of these jobs could be done from home. Only about half the people in these jobs, however, will decide they want to work at home.

'Good teleworkers have high self-esteem and enough money. They do not panic about an irregular income and they feel safe working at home. Their physical needs are well catered for and they belong to a supportive family or friendship group. Such people are now seeking self-fulfilment. They are proud of what they do and what's more, they don't care what others think. They are secure in themselves.'

It amused Moffat that, although her neighbours knew she worked from home much of the time, they did not take this seriously until a film crew arrived to film her for the television program *Beyond 2000*.

The perception or attitude of others can have a big effect on home-based workers. 'A guy in Canberra told me he had worked from home for two years and was dying to get back to a city office. "The newsagent thinks I am unemployed as I go in during the day, the neighbours feel sorry for me . . . I'm fed up with it all," he moaned. Awareness is changing, here as in America. Home-based workers are looked on as being totally professional and providing very good value for money.' In fact the British company for which she worked now has a turnover of $100 million and is regarded as a role model for home-based business. But until this positive perception is widespread Moffat suggests 'shamming it' in some situations. 'If you feel a client will freak out and you won't get the job, don't say you are a home-based worker. I do not invite clients to my home. Instead we use an office in North Sydney with a plush boardroom. In Australia we need to look more closely at measuring productivity—output—rather than merely whether someone is in the office between 9 and 5. This is happening gradually. Big companies are in the early stages of setting policies and guidelines. But working from home will increase as people seek a more flexible lifestyle and companies seek increased productivity.

'When you are working away from the office, the work you are doing has to be better defined. If you are in the office and don't understand what the boss wants, you can talk to others. At home there is no one to ask, you have to know.

'People working from home feel they are being given a privilege, so they tend to work harder to keep that privilege. In addition, research shows that 50 per cent of time in the office is spent in socialising, game-playing and politicking.' Remove those elements and it is little wonder those working from home are far more productive!

Final words

Margaret Seedsman, National Executive Director of Home-Based Business Australia, says home-based business has the potential to help people fulfil their dreams. 'It can offer a lifestyle and work combination not previously thought of, and it can bring greater happiness, as people are doing what they love doing.

'Working from home is taking the ultimate responsibility. Instead of depending on or blaming others, *you* are responsible for generating your own revenue instead of becoming a burden on society,' she says.

So what are you waiting for? Get out of that city office and come back home!

10

USEFUL CONTACTS

Government business centres

Queensland

Queensland Business Information Centre: Floor 21, 111 George Street, GPO Box 1141, Brisbane 4001, tel: 07 3221 1620, fax: 07 3234 0024

New South Wales

Small Business Development Group: Department of State and Regional Development, Level 43, 225 George Street, Grosvenor Place, Sydney 2000, PO Box N818, Grosvenor Place, Sydney NSW 1220, tel: 02 9242 6684, fax: 02 9242 6705

Northern Territory

Department of Asian Relations, Trade and Industry: Business Advisory Services, 76 The Esplanade, Darwin 0801, GPO Box 4160, Darwin 0801, tel: 08 8999 5210, fax: 08 8999 7924

South Australia

The Business Centre: 145 South Terrace, Adelaide 5001, GPO Box 1565, Adelaide 5001, tel: 08 8233 4600, fax: 08 8231 1199

Western Australia

Small Business Development Corporation: 553 Hay Street, Perth 6001, GPO Box C111, Perth 6001, tel: 09 325 3388, fax: 09 221 1132

Tasmania

Tasmania Development and Resources: Small Business Service, 22 Elizabeth Street, Hobart 7000, tel: 03 6233 5888, fax: 03 6233 5800
Tasmania Development and Resources: Small Business Service, 22 Earl Street, Launceston 7250, tel: 03 6336 2501, fax: 03 6334 1131
Tasmania Development and Resources: Small Business Service, PO Box 672, Burnie 7320, tel: 03 6434 6312, fax: 03 6431 9164

Victoria

Small Business Victoria: 215 Spring Street, Melbourne 3000, tel: 03 9655 3300, local toll free: 1800 136034, fax: 03 9651 9725

Non-government centre (government funded)

Australian Capital Territory

Business Link: PO Box 192, Deakin West, ACT 2600, tel: 06 282 2199, fax: 06 282 5045

Chambers of commerce

Queensland

Queensland Chamber of Commerce and Industry: Industry House, 375 Wickham Terrace, Brisbane 4000, tel: 07 3842 2222, fax: 07 3832 3195

New South Wales

State Chamber of Commerce, New South Wales: Level 12, 83 Clarence Street, Sydney 2001, GPO Box 4280, Sydney 2001, tel: 02 9350 8100, fax: 02 9350 8199

Northern Territory

Northern Territory Chamber of Commerce and Industry Incorporated: Suite 5, 2 Shepherd Street, Darwin 0801, GPO Box 1825, Darwin 0801, tel: 08 8981 5755, fax: 08 8981 1405

South Australia

South Australian Employers Chamber of Commerce and Industry Incorporated: Enterprise House, 136 Greenhill Road, Unley 5061, tel: 08 8373 1422, fax: 08 8272 9662

Western Australia

Chamber of Commerce and Industry of Western Australia: 190 Hay Street, East Perth 6604, GPO Box 6209, East Perth 6892, tel: 08 9365 7555, fax: 08 9365 7550

Tasmania

Tasmanian Chamber of Commerce and Industry. 30 Burnett Street, North Hobart 7000, tel: 03 6234 5933, fax: 03 6231 1278
Launceston Chamber of Commerce and Industry: 68 York Street, Launceston 7250, GPO Box 1490, Launceston 7250, tel: 03 6334 6300, fax: 03 6334 6400
Burnie Chamber of Commerce and Industry: GPO Box 139, Burnie 7320, tel: 03 6431 1622

Australian Capital Territory

ACT Chamber of Commerce and Industry Limited: 12A Thesiger Court, Deakin, ACT 2600, PO Box 192, Deakin West, ACT 2600, tel: 06 280 5029, fax: 06 282 2436

Mitchell-Gungahlin Chamber of Commerce Incorporated: PO Box 24, Mitchell 2911, tel: 06 241 3588, fax: 06 241 4193

Victoria

Australian Chamber of Commerce and Industry: Level 4, 55 Exhibition Street, Melbourne 8003, GPO Box 18008, Melbourne 8003, tel: 03 9289 5289, fax: 03 9289 5250

Australian marketing institute branches

Queensland

1st floor, 93–105 Margaret Street, Brisbane 4000, tel: 07 3221 3664, fax: 07 3229 4172

New South Wales

PO Box 373, St Leonards 2065, tel: 02 9438 2433, fax: 02 9438 3800

South Australia

224 Hindley Street, Adelaide 5000, tel: 08 8231 6308, fax: 08 8410 1383

Western Australia

11 Heather Road, Lesmurdie 6076, tel: 09 291 0031

Tasmania

PO Box 1223M, Hobart 7001, tel: 1800 240 264, 03 6224 2244

Victoria

Level 2, 464 St Kilda Road, Melbourne 3004, tel: 03 9821 4444, fax: 03 9820 8650

Standards Australia information centres

Queensland

67 St Pauls Terrace, PO Box 290, Spring Hill 4000, tel: 07 3831 8605, fax: 07 3832 2140

New South Wales

Head Office: 1 The Crescent, Homebush 2140, PO Box 1055, Strathfield 2135, tel: 02 9746 4700, fax: 02 9746 8450; 51 King Street, Newcastle 2300, tel: 049 29 2477, fax: 049 29 3540

Northern Territory

Territory Construction Association (agency): 191 Stuart Highway, Parap 0820, tel: 08 8981 9666, tel/fax: 08 8941 0275

South Australia

63 Greenhill Road, Wayville 5034, tel: 08 8373 4140, fax: 08 8373 4124

Western Australia

1274 Hay Street, West Perth 6005, tel: 09 321 8797, fax: 09 321 2929

Tasmania

Suite 2, 237 Elizabeth Street, North Hobart 7000, tel: 03 6231 5885, fax: 03 6231 5886

Victoria

19–25 Raglan Street, South Melbourne 3205, tel: 03 9693 3533, fax: 03 9696 1319

Australian Capital Territory

Shop 5, Level 4, The Boulevard, Canberra 2601, tel: 06 249 8990, fax: 06 249 8989

Franchise Association of Australia and New Zealand (FAANZ)

FAANZ National Secretariat: Suite 9, 2–6 Hunter Street, Parramatta 2150, tel: 02 9891 4933, fax: 02 9891 4474

Queensland

93–105 Margaret Street, Brisbane 4000, tel: 07 3221 2594

New South Wales

PO Box Q841, QVB Post Office 1230, te: 02 9264 4077

South Australia

55 Henley Beach Road, Mile End 5031, tel: 08 843 3000

Western Australia

229 Adelaide Terrace, Perth 6000, tel: 09 221 5177

Victoria

GPO Box 1498N, Melbourne 3001, tel: 03 9650 1667

Home-based Business Associations

National

Home Business Hotline, tel: 1900 160 066

Victoria

Home-Based Business Australia: 45 Wattle Road, Hawthorn 3122, tel: 03 9818 8344, fax: 03 9818 8450

New South Wales

Business From Home: Level 3, 169 Macquarie Street, Parramatta 2150, tel: 02 9689 1977, fax: 02 9687 0210

South Australia

Home-Bis Incorporated: c/o The Business Centre, 145 South Terrace, Adelaide 5000, tel: 08 8233 4600, fax: 08 8231 1199

Bi-monthly national magazine

HomeBiz: PO Box 503, Chelsea, Vic., 3196, tel: 03 9776 1344, fax: 03 9776 1337

RECOMMENDED READING

The Franchisee's Guide, Martin Mendelsohn, Franchisors Association of Australia and New Zealand Limited, fifth edn, 1996

The Cutting Edge. Jim's Mowing: A Franchise Story, Jim Penman, Australia, 1992

Feel The Fear And Do It Anyway, Susan Jeffers, Random Century, 1989

Get Out of Debt and Prosper!, A 10-step Plan that Really Works, Peter Cutler, Thorsons, 1991

Financially Free, Ann Hartley, Transworld, Moorebank NSW, 1990

Debt Free, Ann Hartley, Transworld, Moorebank NSW, 1992

The Psychology of Money, Ann Hartley, Transworld, Moorebank NSW, 1995

The Richest Man in Babylon, George S. Clason, Signet, New York, 1932

Eating for Peak Performance, Rosemary Stanton, Allen & Unwin, Sydney, 1988

Nutrition for Life, Catherine Saxelby, Reed Books, Australia, 1986

Learned Optimism, Martin E.P. Seligman, Random House, Australia, 1991

Being Happy, Andrew Matthews, Media Masters, Singapore, 1988

The Seven Habits of Highly Effective People, Stephen R. Covey, The Business Library, Victoria, 1990

Thick Face, Black Heart, Chin-Ning Chu, Allen & Unwin, Sydney, 1995
Why Don't People Listen?, Hugh Mackay, Pan Macmillan, Australia, 1994
You and Stress, Dr Bob Montgomery and Lynette Evans, Nelson, Victoria, 1984
Coping with Stress, Dr Bob Montgomery, Pitman, Melbourne, 1982
Managing Stress, The Stress Survival Guide for Today, Ursula Markham, Element, Dorset, United Kingdom, 1989
Stress—How Your Diet Can Help, Stephen Terrass, Thorsons, London, United Kingdom, 1994
Amanda Gore's Stress Busters, Amanda Gore, Lifestyle Press, Sydney NSW, 1991
The Relaxation & Stress Reduction Workbook, Martha Davis, Elizabeth Robbins Eshelman and Matthew McKay, New Harbinger Publications, California, 1995
From Bedlam to Bliss—The Complete Home Organisation System, Wendy Shiels, Random House Australia, 1995
Retirement: A Survey, Professor Sol Encel and Helen Studewcki, New South Wales Consultative Committee on Ageing, 1996

INDEX

Conditions of Entry

1. Send your entry, with contact details, to Home Office Competition, Allen & Unwin Pty Ltd, PO Box 8500, St Leonards, NSW 2065. Entries close at 5pm, Monday, 29 September 1997. A maximum of two entries only from each return address will be considered.
2. Your contact details must include the type of your business.
   ☐ Construction/Manufacturing ☐ Education/Health/Community Services ☐ Retail ☐ Wholesale/Transport/Imports ☐ Finance/Property/Business Services ☐ Other
3. Employees (and their immediate families) of Allen & Unwin Pty Ltd, Officeworks Superstores Pty Ltd and their related companies may not enter.
4. The first and only prize is office equipment and furniture with a retail value of $6,000, selected from Officeworks Superstores Pty Ltd.
5. The promoter is Allen & Unwin Pty Ltd (ACN 003 994 278), PO Box 8500, St Leonards, NSW 2065. The determination of the winner by the promoter shall be binding and final, and no correspondence will be entered into.
6. The winner will be notified in writing, and the result published in the *Australian* newspaper on Friday, 24 October 1997.